ABRAHAM LINCOLN AND KARL MARX IN DIALOGUE

DIALOGUES IN HISTORY

Series Editors
Peter Charles Hoffer
Williamjames Hull Hoffer

Peter Charles Hoffer   *Benjamin Franklin Explains the Stamp
                        Act to Parliament, 1766*

Stephen Berry   *A House Dividing: The Lincoln–Douglas
                        Debates of 1858*

Allan Kulikoff   *Abraham Lincoln and Karl Marx in Dialogue*

Abraham Lincoln and Karl Marx in Dialogue

ALLAN KULIKOFF

Oxford University Press is a department of the University of Oxford. It furthers the University's objective of excellence in research, scholarship, and education by publishing worldwide. Oxford is a registered trade mark of Oxford University Press in the UK and certain other countries.

Published in the United States of America by Oxford University Press
198 Madison Avenue, New York, NY 10016, United States of America.

© Oxford University Press 2018

All rights reserved. No part of this publication may be reproduced, stored in a retrieval system, or transmitted, in any form or by any means, without the prior permission in writing of Oxford University Press, or as expressly permitted by law, by license, or under terms agreed with the appropriate reproduction rights organization. Inquiries concerning reproduction outside the scope of the above should be sent to the Rights Department, Oxford University Press, at the address above.

You must not circulate this work in any other form
and you must impose this same condition on any acquirer.

Library of Congress Cataloging-in-Publication Data
Names: Kulikoff, Allan, author.
Title: Abraham Lincoln and Karl Marx in dialogue / Allan Kulikoff.
Description: New York, NY : Oxford University Press, 2018. |
Series: Dialogues in history | Includes bibliographical references and index.
Identifiers: LCCN 2017026456 (print) | LCCN 2017038890 (ebook) |
ISBN 9780190844653 (Updf) | ISBN 9780190844660 (Epub) |
ISBN 9780190844646 (hardcover) | ISBN 9780190210809 (pbk.)
Subjects: LCSH: Lincoln, Abraham, 1809–1865—Political and social views. |
Marx, Karl, 1818–1883—Political and social views. | United States—History—Civil War, 1861–1865—Economic aspects. | United States—History—Civil War, 1861–1865—Influence. | United States—Economic conditions—19th century. | United States—Social conditions—19th century. | Slavery—Economic aspects—United States.
Classification: LCC E457.2 (ebook) | LCC E457.2 .K85 2017 (print) |
DDC 973.7092—dc23
LC record available at https://lccn.loc.gov/2017026456

For my mentors, teachers, and colleagues:
Lois Green Carr, Stan Engerman, David Fischer, Betsy Fox-Genovese, and Al Young

Contents

Editor's Preface {ix}
Acknowledgments {xi}

Introduction: The Corporate Lawyer and the Revolutionary {1}
Chapter 1: Land and Opportunity in Antebellum America {17}
Chapter 2: Slavery as a Social System {30}
Chapter 3: Secession and the Civil War: Lincoln, Secession, and the Border States {46}
Chapter 4: Slavery, Emancipation, and the Progress of the Civil War, 1861–1862 {64}
Chapter 5: Emancipation and Its Discontents {81}
Chapter 6: Marx and Lincoln on the Fruits of the Civil War {100}
Epilogue: Marx and Lincoln after the Defeat of the Paris Commune {116}

Bibliographic Essay {119}
Notes {125}
Illustration Credits {131}
Index {133}

Editor's Preface

OVER THE PAST several decades, the internationalization of United States history has proceeded apace. Historians understand that North America has always been part of a complex Atlantic world economic and political system, and they want to relay this vision to their students. Focused intensely on national developments, however, historians of antebellum and Civil War America have, until quite recently, dealt almost exclusively with internal developments. Important recent books on the global cotton trade and the international Civil War will help change that perspective. This book provides another thrust in a more global history of the era.

When they think about the Civil War era, students envision generals, battles, and perhaps politics, but ignore its global significance. This book will help undergraduates re-envision the Civil War era in an international perspective. Slavery, historians tell their students, was the fundamental political issue of the 1850s and 1860s and the cause of the Civil War. But the issue of labor—both slavery and free labor—permeated politics throughout the capitalist Atlantic world. Just as Americans supported the European revolutions in 1848, Europeans knew about slavery and abolition and closely followed the progress of the Civil War. European governments and citizens alike chose sides in the war.

Slavery and free labor are the central themes of the documents in this volume. In particular, they emphasize free land for farmers, pro-slavery legislation and anti-slavery politics, the ways slaves freed themselves during the Civil War, and the genesis of and reaction to the Emancipation Proclamation in both the United States and Great Britain. Materials reprinted here come from the newer, nineteenth-century media in the United States and England—mass circulation newspapers, published maps and prints, political speeches, and political organizing and rallies.

Most documents in this collection were chosen from Lincoln's and Marx's voluminous writings. They emphasize this problem of labor relations in the nineteenth-century world. Electronic editions, cited in the bibliography, helped uncover the most significant works, as did the documents Robin Blackburn published in his

An Unfinished Revolution. Both men not only wrote (and spoke) at great length but also very repetitiously. The format of the Oxford Dialogues series provides an opportunity to illuminate key arguments, while excluding extraneous material, and combining maps and illustrations that place Lincoln's and Marx's arguments in a broader social and political context.

Why put Abraham Lincoln and Karl Marx together in the same volume? The Republican and the Communist appear to be strange bedfellows. But that Cold War vision misses the fluid and ambiguous nature of nineteenth-century Atlantic politics. Although their views on labor, class, and politics did conflict, Lincoln and Marx dealt with the same issues and surprisingly often came to similar conclusions about both slavery and the meaning of the Civil War. They both knew, for instance, that the Civil War would end slavery, even if the stated goals of the Union appeared to deny this. The differences they did have, key issues in this volume, illuminate the difficult decisions both men had to make and their quite different social positions.

This book goes beyond the rhetorical beauty of Lincoln's most famous addresses to his everyday prose of governing and to the political calculations required to keep the country together. Those who know Marx only through a cursory reading of the *Communist Manifesto* will be surprised to read his journalism, articles that delved deeply into politics, in ways that resemble today's political debates. In particular, Marx thought that the proletarian revolution could only come about after the victory of the bourgeoisie and—in the case of the United States—after the end of slavery.

All documents in this volume retain the spelling and punctuation found in the original texts. These spellings and conventions may differ from those of the twenty-first century, but they help capture the character of nineteenth-century rhetoric; in particular, the author has retained nineteenth-century uses of derogatory words for people of African descent.

Acknowledgments

This book has had a long genesis; it is the latest act in my search for explanations in the history of American society. For close to a half-century, I have studied American society, particularly that of early America. My focus has been on class, on slavery and slave societies, and on agrarian and urban life, mostly in the eighteenth century. Karl Marx's writings, and those of his twentieth-century historian followers, have long been central to my analysis.

When I entered graduate school some forty-eight years ago, the new social history was becoming ascendant, but Marxist explanations had fallen out of favor. To try and understand American development theoretically, I took a social theory field and read every significant nineteenth-century social theorist, but Karl Marx was conspicuously absent. During the decade after I left graduate school, I learned the importance of Marx and Marxist analysis. Sean Wilentz introduced me to much of the vibrant (if often hidden) controversies among British Marxists. Around the same time, the late Betsy Fox-Genovese showed me how to incorporate class analysis and issues of gender into studies of slave society. Through example and enthusiasm, the late Al Young pushed me toward a less structural kind of people's history, one that emphasized human relations and peoples' life stories. I continued discussions of Marx, class, and slavery with the late Marvin Rosen, and with Jim Schmidt, Terry Thomas, Michael Kwass, Stephen Mihm, and Jake Short. Closer to home, I have discussed political issues, class, and Marx with my wife Lihong Xie and her Chinese friends and with my daughter Xie Rachel Kulikoff; their views have informed my arguments in many ways.

I view the nineteenth century through the lens of the eighteenth century: Lincoln and Marx can both be viewed as Enlightenment figures, men with a deep understanding of the age of the democratic revolutions that took place in their parents' generation. I learned much about the Civil War era three decades ago, when I co-taught a graduate seminar at Princeton in Antebellum and Civil War history with Jim McPherson. Reading for that course combined military, political, and social history.

My graduate students have helped with that education. I have assigned Marx in graduate courses at Northern Illinois University and at the University of Georgia and have often learned from the informed comments students made. My Chinese graduate students at Nankai University and the University of Georgia, Dong Yu and Du Dan foremost among them, introduced me to Chinese visions of Marx. Three years ago, my PhD student Alisha Cromwell organized a History of Capitalism workshop, where a few faculty members and grad students read the entire volume 1 of *Capital*. Despite my long interest in Marx, that was the first time I had gotten through the entire volume, and with it my deeper understanding of Marx's thought.

When I suggested to my colleague Peter Hoffer that I might want to contribute a volume on Lincoln and Marx to his Oxford Dialogues in History series, he encouraged me to do so and made helpful suggestions along the way. Steve Berry provided suggestions for documents and issues and answered questions about the Civil War era, and Stan Engerman raised questions on the penultimate version of the book that improved the clarity of my arguments.

At Oxford University Press, Brian Wheel has been an insightful acquisitions editor, expressing enthusiasm for the project at every stage and making astute suggestions for improvements. Susan Ferber, who took over the manuscript, ably handled the final version through production. Finally, I would like to thank India Gray and the anonymous readers for Oxford University Press who provided substantial help in revising the manuscript.

ABRAHAM LINCOLN AND KARL MARX IN DIALOGUE

INTRODUCTION

The Corporate Lawyer and the Revolutionary

IN 1864, KARL MARX, an impoverished, and sometimes destitute, German-born intellectual and revolutionary living in exile in London, sent a letter to an American politician and lawyer, Abraham Lincoln. The letter congratulated Lincoln on his reelection to the American presidency. Through British Ambassador Charles Francis Adams (son of abolitionist and former president John Quincy Adams), Lincoln responded to the letter with great courtesy. This letter, composed in the name of an English workingman's group, opens a window on nineteenth-century America. It connected the rapidly expanding American empire to its roots across the Atlantic Ocean and hints at the different social and political systems of the United States, the Confederacy, England, France, and German states. It illuminates slavery, the Civil War, and emancipation as well as the development of free labor in workshops and factories in the United States, Great Britain, and continental Europe. Only a few specialists in the history of capitalism know about this exchange, perhaps because the admirers of each man find it embarrassing. Only one book puts the writings of the two men side by side, allowing systematic comparison of their views.[1]

Lincoln and Marx would appear to have had little in common, yet both wrote extensively about politics and society in the United States. By the outbreak of the Civil War in 1861, both had been thinking about the most momentous social forces of their time—slavery and freedom, free labor and exploitation, debasement and economic opportunity—for decades. These were the most crucial political, social, and economic issues through North *and* South America, Great Britain *and* France, German states *and* the Hapsburg Empire.

Posterity would remember both men. Lincoln, the son of a ne'er-do-well farmer, had become a rich lawyer, served one term in the House of Representatives, lost a senatorial election after debating Democrat Stephen Douglas, won the 1860 presidential election exclusively from northern voters, led the Union in the American Civil War, and signed the Emancipation Proclamation. Marx, born into a rich German family, attended college and later received one of the first PhDs granted in philosophy, wrote complex tomes on political economy, fell into genteel poverty, worked as

1

Karl Marx in London

a journalist to feed his family (but received much financial support from his friend and colleague Frederick Engels), wrote polemical tracts to unite the European proletariat, and led the fractured communist movement at its birth. The one suffered a martyr's death and became in popular lore the "Great Emancipator"; the other was revered in one half the twentieth-century world and reviled in the other.

Extant images of the two men build on their contemporary reputations. Marx struggled with genteel poverty his entire adult life. He pictured himself as both an intellectual and a revolutionary. The photo reproduced in this chapter shows him as a shabby gentleman, perhaps dressed in his best clothes, the ones he would wear when reading at the British Library, not those of a working man. The print of "Lincoln the Rail-splitter," made for the 1860 election, turned Lincoln back into a farm laborer, a job he had long abandoned for legal work. This ideological image

Lincoln the Rail-splitter, 1860

painted him as a simple, hard-working, virtuous American rather than as the lawyer and politician he had become.

Though Lincoln may have read some of the pieces Marx wrote for the *New-York Tribune*, and Marx followed Lincoln closely during the Civil War, they never met nor did they exchange any more than the workingmen's congratulation. But Lincoln's administration sought support from British and European workers familiar with Marx. Marx considered emigrating to New York, the city with the third-largest German-speaking population, but—lacking funds for passage—never went there.[2] He nonetheless kept up to date on American affairs by reading works on the United States and the northern and southern US press, and learned about American working conditions and socialist organizations from friends who had emigrated to America.

Placing Lincoln and Marx in dialogue with each other illuminates critical issues in the mid-nineteenth-century Western world. Could slavery and freedom coexist in the United States and elsewhere? Did the Civil War concern slavery or the independence of states held back by overweening national power? What would the end of slavery mean for the United States—and for workers and capitalists throughout the world? How could societies prevent (or should they prevent) the debasement of workers? What was the relationship between the abolition of slavery and the success of the white working class? Did the "free land," found in the Americas and Australia, ready to be taken from the original inhabitants, allow ordinary men to procure property and avoid debased wage labor?

FREE LABOR, SLAVERY, AND THE RIGHTS OF WORKERS

Marx and Lincoln agreed that the rights of labor stood at the center of prosperity, political rights, and progress. Both championed the Union in the Civil War and wanted to rid the United States of slavery. But their agreement stopped there. One defended railroads and, on rare occasions, slaveholders, in court; the other lambasted capitalists and their bourgeois supporters though recognizing that only the capitalists' victory over aristocrats could lead to a workers' revolution. Lincoln saw the unity of labor and capital and insisted all laborers could become prosperous; class conflict between capitalists, who forced workers into a kind of wage slavery, and the workers they exploited stood at the center of Marx's writings.[3]

Lincoln espoused a "free labor" ideology. Families prospered best in societies with free soil (slavery prohibited), free labor (no one held in bondage worked the land), and free men (all men had formal freedom). Although seeking the support of white workingmen, the Republicans thought a capitalist social system, one that provided opportunities and social mobility for free men, allowed them to achieve economic independence, the most ideal society. "Labor" encompassed businessmen and farmers as well as wage workers; class conflict between capitalists and wage workers did not exist.[4] During the Civil War, the Emancipation Proclamation, the Thirteenth Amendment to the Constitution (which outlawed slavery), the Homestead Act (which gave free land to settlers), and the Morrill Act (which established land-grant colleges) put the free labor ideology into practice. Lincoln wrote the Emancipation Proclamation, championed the Homestead and Morrill Acts, and eventually supported the Thirteenth Amendment.

Unlike Lincoln, who saw the United States as an agrarian and small-town nation, Marx knew that industrialization was inevitable. Marx emphasized that the industrial Revolution in England and the United States, the largest industrial powers in the world, caused conflicts between the classes of capitalists and proletarians. The victory of the bourgeoisie (capitalists and their allies) over landed aristocrats would improve human conditions. He (and Engels) wrote lyrically in the *Communist Manifesto* about capitalists who had invented ever-more productive machines and devised the most productive, dynamic, and efficient industrial system the world had seen. But it came at a cost: the transformation of labor into a commodity he called "labor power," which resulted in the oppression of working people. To survive, working people had to sell their labor power to capitalists who stole the "surplus value" they created by their labor (the value they added to raw materials), leaving them with a wage below their subsistence needs. Only by mounting a proletarian revolution that abolished this commodification of people (what economists call labor markets), could machines be harnessed to benefit workers and their families rather than the capitalists. The growth of a working class, what he called a proletariat, in large American cities, like New York, he concluded, would lead to class conflict.

Lincoln had worked without wage compensation on his father's farm until age twenty-one, then lived in towns, and trained for the law; but he nonetheless adhered to a rural, market-oriented version of the ideal of the "self-made man," the idea that hard work would inevitably lead to success, as long as a man remained sober and industrious. In an 1859 speech before the Wisconsin State Agricultural Society, he attacked the "mud-sill theory" of northern "wage slavery" espoused by supporters of slavery such as South Carolina Senator James Henry Hammond. This theory deemed slavery superior to free labor, because slave owners cared for their slaves as members of their families but capitalists debased free workers.

In contrast to Marx, Lincoln argued that northern agrarian society, with its interconnected market economy, provided great opportunities for anyone who cultivated the land intensively. An educated youth improved crops and cultivation methods, and used machinery. He might begin life as a laborer, but as he worked, he accumulated capital, bought tools, and finally got land. The farmer was thus neither capitalist nor laborer; by working on his own land, he shared characteristics of both classes. After the farmer worked his land for a while, he had enough money to hire a wage laborer—and the process of wealth accumulation began anew. Twentieth-century historians called this a "farm ladder"; Lincoln thought it was an enduring characteristic of the northern economy.[5]

For decades, the Democratic Party of Jefferson and Jackson had supported making public land as free as possible to farmers. They championed cheap land prices and pre-emption, the doctrine that those who squatted on land had the first right to purchase it. In these ways, the Democratic Party tried to make universal land ownership by free, white men a reality. Democrats dropped the proposal in the 1850s because southern supporters thought it would increase opposition to slavery. In his one term in Congress, Lincoln's Whig Party had opposed such policies, fearing that they allowed lazy men to steal land and encouraged land speculation. The new Republican Party took up the cry of free land. In 1862 Congress passed and Lincoln signed the Homestead Act, which provided a material base for Lincoln's "farm ladder" by giving every farmer a 160-acre quarter section of federal land—as long as he improved it. Later historians agreed, arguing that the American frontier was a "safety valve" for urban masses.[6]

Although Marx understood that Americans had more opportunities to acquire land than European peasants, he viewed land through the lens of England, where landlords had confiscated peasant land. Land ownership, Marx insisted, would not solve the growing problem of debasement in American cities. In 1846 he calculated that if the United States divided the 1.4 billion acres of open land then in the country into free 160-acre plots, and the American population continued growing rapidly, the land would disappear in four decades. The dream that every farmer would own land, enjoying the fruits of his labor, was as realistic as a proposal to turn everyman into an emperor or king. Moreover, rich northern farmers, Marx wrote in 1862 or 1863, along with slave-owning cotton, rice, and sugar planters controlled the country's agricultural wealth. Notwithstanding this criticism, Marx celebrated the passage of the Homestead Act, perhaps reasoning that the rapid diminishment of free land would thrust most Americans into the proletariat and bring proletarian revolution closer.

SLAVERY AND THE COMING OF SECESSION

Antebellum Americans divided on the future of slavery. Slaves wanted freedom; free blacks in the North espoused universal abolition, decried colonization, and demanded social and political equality for themselves and for the slaves. White Southerners—intellectuals, slaveholders, and poor whites—agreed that slavery was good for slaves and their masters. Northern whites split into three groups: some agreed with their southern brethren; most urged the eventual end to slavery, compensating masters (usually by requiring those born to slave women to serve an apprenticeship, that resembled indentured servitude, until adulthood), and sending the freed people to Liberia, Haiti, or Central America; a tiny minority (perhaps a thousand of twenty million) demanded immediate abolition that would turn slaves into citizens and compensate them for their involuntary servitude.[7]

Before his election in 1860, Lincoln and the Republican Party demanded that slavery be prohibited from American territories and, like anti-slavery advocates had for decades, supported gradual abolition and the colonization of those freed. During his single term in the House of Representatives, Lincoln had introduced a bill for gradual abolition in the District of Columbia, which would have freed all children born to slave women after January 1, 1850, followed by an indeterminate "apprenticeship."[8]

Marx and Lincoln both opposed slavery, but they thought about it in profoundly different ways. Lincoln viewed slavery through a moral and a political lens, but his vision of slaves, slavery, abolition, and the possibilities of freedom changed markedly over his life. His Kentucky in-laws owned slaves and one even traded slaves. Lincoln, who saw slaves when he visited his relations, defended owners' right to slave labor, even as he came to paint slavery in darker colors, as "a vast moral evil." Unlike abolitionists, he rarely mentioned the whipping slavery entailed, nor did he condemn slaveholders as sinners. As a thirty-two-year-old, taking a steamboat to St. Louis, he described a coffle of slaves he saw, chained together, heading away from their homes in Kentucky. Though he wrote of the horrors of family separation, he still deemed them happy. Fourteen years later, he remembered the incident as a scene of torment and torture, one northern anti-slavery advocates like himself were powerless to change.[9]

During the late 1850s, as he gained a national reputation, Lincoln and other Republicans combined moral revulsion with an understanding that the Constitution prohibited the national government from interfering with slavery in the states. Although the Constitution mandated the return of runaway slaves, Lincoln—like other Republicans—contended that it deemed slaves persons, not property. Only state laws, which the Constitution could not touch, could turn persons into property to be bought and sold. This abolitionist doctrine of "freedom national," adopted at the 1856 Republican convention, pushed Lincoln toward more radical anti-slavery positions.[10]

At best, while at peace, the nation could exclude slavery from the territories that the federal government controlled. In 1848, as a Whig congressman, Lincoln voted for David Wilmot's motion that would have prohibited slavery in territories conquered in the Mexican-American War. Southerners lambasted Wilmot's motion; most northern representatives supported it. Lincoln continued to espouse the anti-slavery cause, arguing in his speech accepting the Illinois nomination in 1858 for the United States Senate that the nation could not continue half-slave, half-free, but that it must eventually become entirely one or the other. If the nation prevented slavery from gaining a foothold in the territories, those lands (once cleansed of Indians) would become preserves for white farmers, who would have to compete with neither slaveholders nor free blacks. He remained inflexible on precluding slavery from the territories after his election as president, even as some Republicans in Congress sought compromise to keep the country together.

Blacks should, Lincoln repeatedly urged, have the natural rights listed in the Declaration of Independence—to live as free people and to enjoy the fruits of their labor. But like many white anti-slavery advocates, he held those of African descent as socially and politically inferior to white citizens. He reiterated this point in the Lincoln-Douglas 1858 senatorial debates and clung to it until the heroism of black Union soldiers and the demands of freed people for political rights led him to change his opinion.[11]

While Lincoln worried about the impact of slavery on the United States, Marx corresponded with German labor leaders who had moved to America and had sought to develop an egalitarian labor movement, open to all, including free blacks. Marx's egalitarianism carried over to his views of slavery. In 1846, Marx linked slavery and mechanized factory labor. He argued that "without slavery you have no cotton, without cotton you have no modern industry." The United States, without slavery and cotton, "would be transformed into a primitive country." Three years later, he defined American slavery in economic terms: a person of African descent became "a *slave* only in certain relationships"; when used to produce cotton, he or she turned into planters' capital.

Marx made similar arguments in *Capital*, which he wrote during the early 1860s. Only staple production, especially cotton, led to overwork, so that masters often used up slaves in a mere seven years, requiring slaveholders to purchase "his laborer as he buys his horse"; losing a slave, he makes a "new outlay in the slave market." (Marx may have elided West Indian sugar plantations, where newly arrived African slaves died in great numbers with those in the United States.) Although this might describe eighteenth-century West Indian and Brazilian sugar cultivation, the US slave population grew rapidly by natural increase, suggesting a less severe labor regime.

Neither Lincoln nor Marx knew about the variety of tasks slaves performed or the rich community life slaves, oppressed as they were, crafted in the decades before the Civil War. Lincoln, who had slave-owner kinfolk and had seen slaves, rarely mentioned slave life in his public pronouncements, limiting himself to broad ideological issues. Lincoln knew that slavery, as a system, encompassed more than the cotton South; Marx—thinking about the largest slaveholders—emphasized cotton and linked slave-produced commodities and the progress of capitalism on both sides of the Atlantic. During the Civil War, Lincoln, along with his Republican colleagues, knew that slaves, longing for freedom, would try to reach Union lines and hoped that this would force Confederate soldiers to return home to do the work their slaves had abandoned.[12]

As the Civil War began, Marx echoed the theme of Lincoln's "House Divided" speech. Instead of using biblical language, he viewed the Civil War as a structural conflict, one between "two systems" that "can no longer live peaceably side by side but can only be ended by the victory of one system or the other."[13] During the war, he supported militant abolitionism and racial equality, arguing that no worker could enjoy freedom (and ultimately rebel against the capitalists who exploited them) unless all, white and black alike, were free.

SLAVERY AND THE CIVIL WAR

The American Civil War looked different from Lincoln's Washington and Marx's London. At the outbreak of the war, Lincoln claimed that the war aimed to preserve the Union, not to abolish slavery, but he knew (as did his Confederate adversaries) that slavery had caused the war. War, Republicans contended, would lead to a bloody and rapid end of slavery, as slaves freed themselves (self-emancipation) by bloody slave rebellions and by running away while the army enticed runaways to help defeat the Confederacy (military emancipation)—rather than the gradual and compensated end they thought exclusion of slavery from the territories would bring. Such military necessity, construed as broadly as possible, Republicans thought, would speed freeing slaves owned by traitorous rebels.[14]

Marx and Lincoln, at first, saw the goals, but perhaps not the results, of the Civil War differently. Lincoln viewed the union formed by the Constitution as a perpetual one; no state had the right to secede. The war aimed to defeat the rebels. Although he wished to ban slavery in the territories, he did not frame the war as one that aimed at emancipation. A few radicals, like abolitionist William Lloyd Garrison, thought he should let the Confederacy go, thereby creating a free nation in the North and West. From the outset, Marx viewed the war as one about slavery—with abolition everywhere as its primary goal, and the liberation of free American workers its ultimate, if distant, consequence. Such liberation would not come easily, since the Union had a form of capitalism, too. But slavery, Marx knew, had buttressed capitalism: slaves cultivated nearly all the cotton that English mills turned into textiles. With slavery gone, workers could organize, across race lines, and demand their rights.

Lincoln knew he had no constitutional power to end slavery. The war, however, allowed him leeway to free slaves of rebellious masters, if those actions helped restore the Union. He insisted that state officials, not national ones, enforce the Fugitive Slave Act, thereby encouraging slaves to escape. Slaves, escaping from masters in the Border States, soon learned they might gain freedom by declaring their masters rebels or themselves free. He looked the other way when abolitionist generals accepted runaway slaves into their camps, as long as soldiers didn't "entice" them. He told Illinois Senator Orville Browning in July 1861 that "the government neither should, nor would send back to bondage such as came to our armies."

Some commanders—appalled at slave catchers in their midst—welcomed runaways to camp, and even received slaves of loyal masters, owners who supported the Union, with the promise that their masters would receive compensation. Others in Maryland and Kentucky returned them to their masters. When General John Fremont, the 1856 Republican candidate for president, freed all slaves of Missouri rebels, not merely those who reached Union lines, Lincoln—fearing the order's impact in Border States—rescinded it. When he fired Fremont for insubordination, abolitionists and even moderate anti-slavery advocates condemned him.[15]

Lincoln sought *both* to keep the slave Border States in the Union *and* to entice slaveholders there to support gradual abolition. Maryland, Kentucky, and Missouri stayed in the Union but suffered much internal conflict, sometimes erupting into civil war. Republicans, Lincoln included, expected slavery would wither away in the Border States. He offered to compensate masters for the slaves they freed and to encourage freed people to leave the country. Even with the threat that they would lose their slaves, without compensation, if they did not accept his offer, every Border State refused. Delaware, with its tiny slave population, declined to consider gradual emancipation bills Lincoln himself wrote. Only in 1864, more than a year after the Emancipation Proclamation, did Missouri and Maryland abolish slavery; Delaware waited until the Thirteenth Amendment was ratified.

From the beginning of the war through late 1862, moderate Republicans, hoping the promise of colonization of freed people abroad would entice Border States to agree to gradual abolition, had espoused colonization; anti-slavery Border State congressmen demanded it. But newly freed slaves rejected emigration, and when Lincoln broached it to a delegation of black leaders, they denounced the idea as enshrining racial inequality. Congress appropriated funds for colonization, but Lincoln knew almost no freed slaves would volunteer, even if they could find countries willing to grant land to them. Once Lincoln signed the Emancipation Proclamation, he ceased to publically support colonization, even as he continued to search for places that might take freed slaves.[16]

Warfare greatly influenced the legal and constitutional constraints on abolition. Even before the war began (but after Lincoln's election), slaves, as much as their masters, understood a Union invasion of the South would mean the possibility of freedom. As the war waged on, Lincoln gradually espoused more vigorous action to free slaves, framing every incident of military emancipation or self-emancipation as a necessary war action. While adhering to constitutional scruples, he signed the first Confiscation Act, a bill defining slaves as "held to labor" rather than property. The law allowed the army to use runaway slave refugees for military purposes, and in March 1862 he signed an order forbidding the army or navy from sending fugitive slaves home. Congress rescinded the Fugitive Slave Act and authorized military commanders to accept slaves into their camps, as long as their masters supported the Confederacy.[17]

When runaways reached Union lines, some military commanders set up camps and fed and sheltered the former slaves. Self-emancipation and military emancipation led Lincoln to expect that before the war ended, most slaves would be freed and states would abolish slavery. Before he issued the Emancipation Proclamation, thousands of slaves fled their masters and took up residence in military camps. By January 1862, freed slaves on Union-occupied Sea Islands refused to work without a guarantee of continued freedom. Capture of lands in the Mississippi River Valley brought thousands more into Union encampments. To accommodate them, Congress passed a second Confiscation Act, allowing military commanders to free any slaves of rebels who reached their camps, even from the Border States or areas the Union controlled. Where masters had abandoned plantations or the Union confiscated them, commanders had the freed slaves paid a monthly wage and received food and clothing rations, an action that rendered continued enslavement, even by loyal masters impossible. The wages hardly provided a subsistence. Nonetheless, if masters refused to pay wages, their slaves would abandon them to work on plantations the Union army controlled. The Act allowed Lincoln to emancipate slaves in areas the Confederacy controlled.[18]

While Lincoln ran a war, Marx, sitting in the British Museum's Library ten hours a day, read every American newspaper (North *and* South), economic tome, and census report he could find. Where Lincoln saw secession as destroying the Union, Marx understood the politics behind the slaveholders' revolution. Marx knew and Lincoln feared that southern leaders would insist on incorporating the southwestern and plains territories into the Confederacy. Prohibiting slavery in the territories, as Lincoln wanted, Marx argued, would destroy the slaveholding system. To preserve slavery required positive national law, but if a majority of the Senate held anti-slavery views, those positive laws and regulations were threatened.[19]

During 1861 and 1862, after his contract with the *New-York Tribune* expired, Marx wrote about the Civil War in Vienna's *Die Presse*. He aimed to inform German-language readers about the abolitionist consequences of a Union victory. Liberal supporters of the failed 1848 revolutions had thought the Confederacy constituted a people rebelling against strong government and imperial tyranny. Like Lincoln early in the war, these European liberals denied that the Civil War aimed at overthrowing slavery.

Marx argued that the Civil War was a struggle between slavery and free labor. Since slavery economically and politically required new territory, Lincoln's election would presage its destruction, even if Republicans claimed to protect it in states where it existed. The Confederate states, a slaveholders' republic, had rebelled *only* to protect slavery. The Civil War pitted 300,000 southern aristocrats (who exploited millions of slaves and most strongly supported secession) against a dynamic, growing economy; a democracy, that—however flawed—held out hope for workers, who could agitate for change or foment revolution. A Union victory in the war, which he expected, would thus inevitably lead to the end of slavery.

Marx followed military orders about abolition and the resulting military emancipation and self-emancipation closely. In late 1861, he told readers in *Die Presse* about the mass movement of runaways to contraband camps, claiming that some fifty thousand had freed themselves in Missouri alone, but he admitted that some military commanders had sent them away. At the same time, masters, fearful their slaves would abscond, took slaves faraway from military action. A half-year later, Marx reported the signing of an Anglo-American treaty meant to suppress the Atlantic slave trade, one he claimed had dealt "a mortal blow" to "the Negro trade."[20]

THE EMANCIPATION PROCLAMATION

In summer 1862, Congress passed the Confiscation Act and abolished slavery in the territories and the District of Columbia, compensating owners as much as $300 for each slave, actions aimed at surrounding slave states with a "cordon of free States," a common metaphor used by abolition-minded Republicans. Runaways from Maryland and Virginia poured into the District. Soon after, Lincoln broached the idea of emancipating slaves in Confederate-held areas as a war measure, allowed by the second Confiscation Act, to his cabinet. He kept quiet about his intentions, hoping to keep the Border States calm. But he did lecture Border State congressmen about the inevitability of war-induced abolition and urged them to support gradual abolition, eliciting fervent opposition from three-quarters of them. In the meantime, support for a presidential proclamation, even among moderate Republicans, grew. Biding his time, Lincoln disingenuously responded to a letter from abolitionist editor Horace Greeley, which urged immediate abolition, by reiterating that he would do whatever proved necessary to preserve the Union even if not a single slave became free. Abolitionists naturally expressed alarm.[21]

After the Union victory at the battle of Antietam, Maryland in September, 1862, Lincoln issued a preliminary Emancipation Proclamation, to take effect on January 1, 1863, if the Confederacy failed to surrender. It would free all slaves living in states and regions then in rebellion and insist they remain free. Confederate states had to reenter the union, end slavery themselves, or suffer the uncompensated loss of their slave workers. Lincoln worded both the preliminary and the final Emancipation Proclamation in legalistic language, justifying military emancipation as a "fit and necessary war measure" and "an act of justice."

The final Proclamation became a military order, circulated to the entire army. In April 1863, the army issued "Instructions for the Government of Armies of the United States in the Field," written by Columbia University professor Francis Lieber at the behest of the secretary of war, as a military order to govern the behavior of Union armies. The instructions codified the Emancipation Proclamation, justifying military emancipation and prohibiting the re-enslavement of those freed, while denying any compensation to their former masters. Slaves, seeing the Union army as an army of liberation, rushed to military camps or readily joined the Union troops who liberated them. Even then, Lincoln reiterated his support for emancipation *and* colonization in his December 1862 annual address to Congress, mystifying and angering his abolitionist supporters.

The final Proclamation immediately freed few people, leaving slaves in the Border States and nearly all areas already recaptured from the Confederacy in bondage. (Some fifty thousand former slaves living in the Union-occupied Sea Islands and other places with few pro-Union whites did gain freedom). It *prospectively* freed some three million slaves living in parts of the Confederacy not yet conquered. Nor did it abolish slavery in the states, which the Constitution forbade. But it allowed ex-slaves, free blacks, and even slaves into the army for the first time since the Revolutionary War. The 180,000 who served, a fifth of the Union army, became essential to subduing the Confederacy. Lincoln's Proclamation, and military orders he approved, encouraged military and self-emancipation, particularly in areas it excluded (such as the Border States), where abolitionist troops enticed slaves to run away by promising them freedom.[22]

Once Lincoln signed the Proclamation, he thought slaves would learn about it through an invisible communications network. He did expect slaves in the affected areas to free themselves. But he admonished them "to abstain from all violence, unless in necessary self-defence" and to "labor faithfully for reasonable wages," that is become wage-laborers, not the farmers he praised in his 1859 Wisconsin Agricultural Society address.

The Emancipation Proclamation had an extraordinary impact on the war. Granted, the process of military emancipation and self-emancipation had begun as soon as the war started. Nonetheless, with the stroke of a pen, the Proclamation changed Lincoln's war aims, aligning him with abolitionist Radical Republicans. It repudiated compensated abolition and gradual abolition in the areas still in rebellion, while including all slaves, even those owned by loyal masters. He thought it the "central act of my administration and the great event of the nineteenth century."[23]

Marx immediately understood the importance of the Emancipation Proclamation, writing to Engels that southern fury had proved its significance. Nor did the legalistic language of the Proclamation diminish its "historic content." Marx was right: after the Union army arrived, the Proclamation incited some 400,000 slaves to run away, most young men rather than families, and led 180,000 slaves and free blacks to enlist; a total of a fifth of black men under forty-five enlisted. The Proclamation, the continuing war, and the actions of the runaways led Lincoln to abandon colonization of the freed people and come closer to the vision of abolitionists. By the end of the war, the military and the Proclamation freed about 525,000 slaves, less than one out of seven of those held in bondage: planters moved slaves away from the war, and, when that didn't work, patrols killed slaves who dared leave. Even successful runaway slaves might suffer re-enslavement in areas the Confederacy recaptured. Only ratification of the Thirteenth Amendment to the Constitution, which outlawed slavery, fully achieved abolition.[24]

THE VIEW FROM LONDON: SLAVES AND WORKERS

In the name of British workers, Marx composed a letter congratulating Lincoln and the American people on his reelection. Even though the Union blockade threw many of them out of work, British workers had long supported the Union, holding meetings and passing pro-Union resolutions. Marx may have organized the most famous of these meetings, the London Trades Council in March 1863, one that united liberals, workers, and socialists; the group invited Ambassador Charles Francis Adams, who sent his son Henry.[25]

The International Working Men's Association, a British and French trade union movement, asked him to compose the letter to Lincoln. He fully expected that Lincoln, who had made "resistance to the Slave Power" the "watchword of your first election," would turn "Death to Slavery" into "the triumphant war cry of your reelection." Marx then reprised his analysis of secession and connected the slave power to workers, in America and Europe. The South's "300,000 slaveholders" had "dared to inscribe for the first time . . . 'slavery' on the banner of Armed Revolt," on the same soil where their ancestors had formed the first "great Democratic Republic." The counter-revolutionaries had "maintained slavery to be a 'beneficent institution,' and indeed the only solution of the great problem of 'the relation of labor to capital.'"

Marx insisted that the Confederacy, far from favoring workers, had supported the "holy crusade of property against labor," leading to the wage slavery American workers suffered. By property, he meant capital—land, rents, financial assets. When northern workers "allowed slavery to defile their own republic," supporting masters' right to sell their slaves, "they boasted the highest prerogative of the white-skinned laborer to sell himself and choose his own master." While slavery continued, they could not "attain the true freedom of labor." European workers knew that just as the American Revolution had "initiated a new era of ascendency for the middle class, so the American Antislavery War will do the same for the working class." Lincoln, "the single-minded son of the working class," Marx concluded, would "lead his country through the matchless struggle for the rescue of an enchained race and the reconstruction of a social world."

Marx crafted the letter brilliantly. He associated the workers' association with Lincoln's policies *and* with Lincoln's vision of the significance of the Emancipation Proclamation. His letter captured Lincoln's ideal of the self-made man. Lincoln, the corporate lawyer turned president, had never been a "son of the working class," but the son of a hard-scrabble farmer, a class closer to the European peasantry than to urban, industrial proletarians. Before his election, he had practiced the quintessential bourgeois occupation of lawyer. By obscuring Lincoln's origins and class, Marx could link Lincoln's war policy with the slaves' struggle to free themselves and the workers' liberation from capitalist exploitation. In Marx's vision, slaves, freed people, white workers, and Lincoln himself were workers or had come from the working class.[26]

Lincoln hoped that the Proclamation would lead to greater support for the Union from Britain and the rest of Europe, particularly that of the working men who Marx claimed to represent. He thus instructed his ambassador to Great Britain, Charles Francis Adams (son and grandson of presidents) to respond. Adams claimed Lincoln had received the letter, along with many others from "friends of humanity and progress throughout the world." Lincoln regarded the war "with slavery-maintaining insurgents as the cause of human nature." For that reason, they "derive new encouragement to persevere from the testimony of the workingmen of Europe," and "with their enlightened approval."

Lincoln's assassination ended Marx's relationship (if one can call it that) with the president. But Marx understood, as did the Radical Republicans in Congress, that the work of reform had barely begun. English workers supported mandating education and granting voting rights to freedmen, as a first step in organizing the working class. Workers soon learned, as did Congress, that President Andrew Johnson was hardly an ally. They would have to mount their protests, allied with American workers, fighting the wealth, ostentation, and federal policies of the Gilded Age. Proletarians would have to free themselves, much as slaves had done.

Reading Marx's and Lincoln's writings alongside one another challenges conventional views that states' rights, constitutionalism, or tariffs rather than slavery led to the outbreak of war. In 1929, Charles Ramsdell published an influential article entitled "The Natural Limits of Slavery Expansion." He insisted that because slavery had a "natural limit" to areas where cotton could be grown, the system could not have expanded into the territories, particularly those on the plains. He thus denied Republican William Seward's 1858 depiction of the conflict as an "irrepressible conflict" between slavery and freedom. In their best-selling 1927 *Rise of American Civilization*, Charles and Mary Beard buttressed this argument. They insisted that economic differences between North and South rather than slavery, led to the Civil War.[27]

Nearly all historians today accept Seward's vision, one that both Marx and Lincoln, albeit in different ways, adhered to. Slavery thrived throughout the South, except in the most isolated and most mountainous areas. The Beards did not understand how closely slavery and economic development were linked. Secession declarations, which mention slavery in nearly every sentence, sustain this view of the war. Northern newspaper editorials thought that war, by eliminating some constraints on government, would inevitably lead to the end of slavery, and Lincoln shared that conclusion.

Marx, writing from London, understood the war more clearly than some of those closer to the ground. From the outset, he knew it concerned slavery. Even as the most fervent abolitionists despaired, he expected a Union victory and knew such a victory would lead to the immediate abolition of slavery. As the war continued, as more and more slaves emancipated themselves, Lincoln came closer to Marx's position on the war's aims and results. No wonder Marx championed the Emancipation Proclamation, for it fully sustained his long-held beliefs about the war and its consequences.

The documents in this collection are divided into six chapters: opportunity in the antebellum North; Marx and Lincoln's views on slavery; the causes of secession and the Civil War; slavery and the Civil War; the Emancipation Proclamation; and Marx's letter to Lincoln. Two chapters deal with the prewar years. Chapter 1 includes Lincoln's 1859 address to the Wisconsin Agricultural Society and excerpts from Marx's journalistic comments on free land. Chapter 2 opens with Lincoln's 1841 and 1855 reactions to the slave coffle and continues with Marx's earliest comments on slavery, excerpts from Lincoln's 1854 Peoria speech and his well-known 1858 "House Divided" speech, in which he accepted the Republican nomination for the US Senate. Marx's short, 1860-1861 musings about slavery and his somewhat later comments on it (1866 in *Capital*), end the chapter.

Chapter 3 compares Lincoln's thoughts on secession before he took office, his interview with pro-slavery editor Duff Green, and his First Inaugural Address, with excerpts from Marx's letters to Engels and his journalism in the *Tribune* and *Die Press* on secession and the coming of the Civil War. Chapter 4 concentrates on the slow progress of the Civil War and its relation to emancipation: it contrasts Marx's continued belief that the war concerned slavery and his demands that Lincoln place emancipation at the center of his policy with Lincoln's slow adoption of that position, ending with his preliminary Emancipation Proclamation and his infamous attempt to get free blacks in Washington, DC to support colonization of freed slaves. Chapter 5 contains the preliminary and final Emancipation Proclamations and his directives to generals to put it into operation, along with Marx's reaction to the Proclamation and to the disappointing results of the 1862 mid-term election. Chapter 6 contains Marx's 1864 address to British workers, the exchange between Marx and Lincoln, Ambassador Charles Francis Adams's response to the letter, Lincoln's last address on Reconstruction in Louisiana, and Marx's musings on the meaning of abolition for workers. A short afterword depicts an 1871 imaginary conversation between Lincoln and Marx about slavery and abolition in a New York City coffeehouse.

CHAPTER 1

Land and Opportunity in Antebellum America

Middling Americans, the vast majority of whom lived in the countryside, expected to own land, but growing minorities could not do so. From the 1830s to the 1850s, land acquisition stood at the center of American politics. The Democratic Party, then the champion of rural, free white American men, worked to make land cheaper, if not free; others demanded workers organize and "vote themselves a farm." Horace Greeley, the radical New-York Tribune *editor, urged the abolition of inheritance and the ready distribution of land to male householders, presumably (but not explicitly) including all heads of household. Karl Marx first wrote about land, opportunity, and the working class in the United States more than a decade before Lincoln addressed the Wisconsin Agricultural Society on the same issue, but Marx thought free land would not solve the growing problems of poverty and dispossession in the United States.*

MARX AND LAND REFORM

Marx and Engels, "The Volks-Tribun's Political Economy."

In 1846, Marx attacked Hermann Kriege, a radical German émigré living in New York City. Kriege espoused land reform as a solution to the problems of the German workers living there. That movement urged the distribution of 160 acres of government-owned land to "every farmer," a goal achieved in the later Homestead Act that Lincoln championed. Marx ridiculed Kriege for assuming that free land would permanently solve America's labor problems.

Marx uses the term "farmer" or "small farmer" as both a class and an occupational term, meaning landowning agriculturalist. "Modern bourgeois society" is Marx's term for the factory labor system of wage laborers and capitalists; the "proletarian movement" is one of workers, who after their struggle with capitalists, would form a communist society. The "American national Reformers" refers to utopian socialist George Evans's National Reform Association—and especially his German immigrant allies—which was made up of men who sought abolition of capitalist land markets, and if that did not work, free land to all citizens.[1]

We fully recognise that the American national Reformers' movement is historically justified. We know that this movement has set its sights on a goal which, although for the moment it would further the industrialism of modern bourgeois society, nevertheless, as the product of a proletarian movement, as an attack on landed property . . . , will by its own inner logic inevitably press on to communism. Kriege . . . , pastes over this plain fact . . . , without ever going into the positive substance of the movement, [and] thereby . . . quite smothers the issue of land-distribution to the small farmer on an American scale . . . .

We read: "They"—that is, the American National Reformers—"call the soil the communal heritage of all mankind . . . and want the legislative power of the people to take steps to preserve as the inalienable communal property of all mankind the 1,400 million acres of land which have not yet fallen into the hands of rapacious speculators." In order communally to "preserve for all mankind" this "communal heritage," this "inalienable communal property," he adopts the plan of the National Reformers: "to place 160 acres of American soil at the command of every farmer, from whatever country he may hail, so that he may feed himself . . . ."

Marx then ridicules Kriege for ignoring differences in land quality and the likelihood that those who acquired better land would soon turn his less lucky neighbor into a laborer.

Kriege . . . considers 160 acres of land as an ever-constant measure, as if the value of such an area did not vary according to its quality. The "farmers" will have to exchange, if not their land itself, then at least the produce of their land, with each other and with third parties, and when this juncture has been reached, it will soon become apparent that one "farmer," even though he has no capital, will, simply by his work and the greater initial productivity of his 160 acres, reduce his neighbour to the status of his farm labourer.

Let us for the moment take Kriege's present to mankind seriously. 1,400 million acres are to be "preserved as the inalienable communal property of all mankind." Specifically, 160 acres are to be the portion of each "farmer." From this we can calculate the size of Kriege's "all mankind"— exactly 8¾ million "farmers," each of whom as head of family represents a family of five, a sum total therefore of 43¾ million people. We can likewise calculate how long "all eternity" will last, for the duration of which "the proletariat in its capacity as humanity" may "claim" "the whole earth"—at least in the United States. If the population of the United States continues to grow at the same rate as hitherto (i.e., if it doubles in 25 years), this "all eternity" will not last out 40 years; within this period the 1,400 million acres will be settled, and there will be nothing left for future generations to "claim." But since the release of the land would greatly increase immigration, Kriege's "all eternity" might well be foreclosed even earlier. The more so when one considers that land for 44 million would not even suffice to channel off the now existing pauper-population of Europe, where every tenth man is a pauper and the British Isles alone supply 7 million . . . .

Deutsche-Brüsseler-Zeitung, *November 11, 1847.*

Marx returned to the issue of land and other productive property a year after his critique of Kriege. Quoting American authorities, he detailed the growth of social inequality and pauperism in a democratic country, thinking it would soon lead to a proletarian revolution. Marx emphasized rural social and economic conflict in industrializing America, something Lincoln denied in his speech before the Wisconsin Agricultural Society.

By "feudal property relations" he refers to systems of land tenure, in which lords demanded tribute from peasants and in return guaranteed their using land; "bourgeois property relations" deals with the land, factories, and financial assets capitalists owned. Marx defined the "bourgeoisie" as the ruling class of societies under industrial capitalism: the factory owners, bankers, and finance capitalists who controlled much of the wealth of the country, along with the lawyers, politicians, and others who did their bidding and ran governments. The contradictions that he thought would ultimately destroy capitalism could be seen, he asserted, most clearly in republics like the United States.[2]

The question of property, depending on the different levels of development of industry, has always been the vital question for a particular class. In the 17th and 18th centuries, when the point at issue was the abolition of feudal property relations, the question of property was the vital question for the bourgeois class. In the 19th century, when it is a matter of abolishing bourgeois property relations, the question of property is a vital question for the working class . . .

The more advanced this society is . . . the further the bourgeoisie has developed economically in a country and therefore the more state power has assumed a bourgeois character, the more glaringly does the social question [about landed property] obtrude itself, in France more glaringly than in Germany, in England more glaringly than in France, in a constitutional monarchy more glaringly than in an absolute monarchy, in a republic more glaringly than in a constitutional monarchy.

Thus, for example, the conflicts of the credit system, speculation, etc., are nowhere more acute than in North America. Nowhere, either, does social inequality obtrude itself more harshly than in the eastern states of North America, because nowhere is it less disguised by political inequality. If pauperism has not yet developed there as much as in England, this is explained by economic circumstances . . . Meanwhile, pauperism is making the most gratifying progress. "In this country, where there are no privileged orders, where all classes of society have equal rights" (the difficulty however lies in the existence of classes) "and where our population is far from . . . pressing on the means of subsistence, it is indeed alarming to find the increase of pauperism progressing with such rapidity." (Report by Mr. Meredith to the Pennsylvania Congress.) "It is proved that pauperism in Massachusetts has increased by three-fifths within 25 years." (*Niles' Register* . . . .)

Despite his critique of American land reformers, Marx nonetheless recognized, in his Eighteenth Brumaire of Louis Bonaparte *and in an 1852 letter to German socialist émigré Joseph Weydemeyer that the class struggle of proletarians and capitalists had not developed as far in the United States as in Britain and that opportunity was much greater than in Europe. In 1851, Engels had written Weydemeyer about "the ease with which the overflow population settles on the land, the necessarily increasing tempo of the country's prosperity which makes people consider bourgeois conditions as a beau ideal." Weydemeyer, horrified by "the shopkeeper's mentality" of American Germans, wrote Marx and Engels that for them every "other aim in life besides making money is considered an absurdity." Marx interpreted this as "constant flux," and reiterated his position in an 1865 manuscript on prices and wages. By "peasants," Marx means what most Americans called farmers.*³

Marx, Eighteenth Brumaire of Louis Bonaparte *(1852).*

[I]n the United States of North America, where, true enough classes already exist, but have not yet acquired permanent character, are in constant flux and reflux, constantly changing their elements . . ., where the modern means of production, instead of coinciding with a stagnant population, rather compensate for the relative deficiency of heads and hands, and where, finally, the feverish, youthful life of material production, which has to appropriate a new world to itself, has so far left neither time nor opportunity left to abolish the illusions of old.⁴

Marx to Weydemeyer, March 1852.

[I]n the United States bourgeois society is still far too immature for the class struggle to be made perceptible and comprehensible; striking proof of this is provided by C. H. [Charles Henry] Carey..., the only North American economist of any note. He attacks [David] Ricardo, the most classic representative of the bourgeoisie and the most stoical opponent of the proletariat, as a man whose works are an arsenal for anarchists and socialists, ... of tearing society apart, and of paving the way for civil war by showing that the economic bases of the various classes are such that they will inevitably give rise to a necessary and ever-growing antagonism between the latter. He tries to refute them ... by seeking to demonstrate that economic conditions: rent (landed property), profit (capital) and wages (wage labour), rather than being conditions of struggle and antagonism, are conditions of association and harmony. All he proves ... is that the "undeveloped" relations in the United States are, to him, "normal relations..."[5]

Marx, Value, Price and Profit *(1865)*.

In colonial countries the law of supply and demand favours the working man. Hence the relatively high standard of wages in the United States. Capital may there try its utmost. It cannot prevent the labour market from being continuously emptied by the continuous conversion of wage labourers into independent, self-sustaining peasants. The position of a wages labourer is for a very large part of the American people but a probational state, which they are sure to leave within a longer or shorter term....[6]

LINCOLN AND FARMERS

Wisconsin Agricultural Society Address.

Abraham Lincoln gave dozens of speeches between 1858 and 1860 on slavery and particularly slavery in the territories, which he sought to prohibit. But in an 1859 address to the Wisconsin Agricultural Society, he turned to farming. Like Marx, he applauded the use of machinery. He championed agricultural improvement—the use of machines, more intensive cultivation, and the need for "book farming" (learning from written materials) as well as brawn. Lincoln does refer to farmers as a "class," a term he uses to mean those who farmed independently, as owners or tenants.[7]

I presume I am not expected to employ the time assigned me, in the mere flattery of the farmers, as a class. My opinion of them is that, in proportion to numbers, they are neither better nor worse than any other class.... But farmers, being the most numerous class, it follows that their interest is the largest interest. It also follows that that interest is most worthy of all to be cherished and cultivated . . . .

My first suggestion is an inquiry as to the effect of greater thoroughness in . . . Agriculture than now prevails in the North-West . . . . [F]ifty bushels of wheat, or one hundred bushels of Indian corn can be produced from an acre . . . . Many years ago I saw it stated in a Patent Office Report that eighteen bushels was the average crop throughout the wheat growing region of the United States; and this year an intelligent farmer of Illinois, assured me that he did not believe the land harvested in that State this season, had yielded more than an average of eight bushels to the acre . . . . As to Indian corn . . . , the case has not been much better. For the last four years I do not believe the ground planted with corn in Illinois, has produced an average of twenty bushels to the acre . . . .

What would be the effect upon the farming interest, to push the soil up to something near its full capacity? Unquestionably it will take more labor to produce fifty bushels from an acre, than it will to produce ten bushes from the same acre. But will it take more labor to produce fifty bushels from one acre, than from five? Unquestionably, thorough cultivation will require more labor to the acre; but will it require more to the bushel? . . . It is certain that thorough cultivation would spare half or more than half, the cost of land, simply because the same product would be got from half, or from less than half the quantity of land . . . .

A great amount of "locomotion" is spared by thorough cultivation. Take fifty bushels of wheat, ready for the harvest, standing upon a single acre, and it can be harvested . . . , with less than half the labor which would be required if it were spread over five acres . . . . It is plain that when the crop is very thick upon the ground, the larger proportion of the power is directly applied to gathering in and cutting it; and the smaller, to that which is totally useless as an end. And what I have said of harvesting is true, in a greater or less degree of mowing, plowing, gathering in of crops generally, and, indeed, of almost all farm work . . . .

The successful application of steam power, to farm work is a desideratum—especially a Steam Plow. It is not enough, that a machine operated by steam, will really plow. To be successful, it must, all things considered, plow better than can be done with animal power. It must do all the work as well, and cheaper; or more rapidly, so as to get through more perfectly in season . . . . I have never seen a machine intended for a Steam Plow . . . . It is to be hoped that the steam plow will be finally successful, and if it shall be, "thorough cultivation"—putting the soil to the top of its capacity—producing the largest crop possible from a given quantity of ground—will be most favorable to it . . . .

Lincoln then turned from farm productivity and equipment to the key part of his speech—an examination of labor systems, North and South. He contrasted the mud-sill theory espoused by pro-slavery advocates, one that deemed slavery the best labor system the world had seen, with the free labor theory. The most vehement proponent of the mud-sill theory, South Carolina Senator James Henry Hammond, told his colleagues that "in all social systems there must be a class to do the menial duties, to perform the drudgery of life." These people—"the very mud-sill of society"— required "but a low order of intellect and but little skill." The South had "found a race adopted to that purpose," one inferior to whites, but in the North the same people were white. Hammond, unlike Lincoln, presumed that nearly all agricultural labor—white as well as black—was debased and unskilled, unworthy of educated people.[8]

Lincoln's insistence that labor proceeded capital and that capital emerged from labor resembled Marx's labor theory of value—but certainly not Marx's theories of surplus value and exploitation that grew out of it. He rejected Marx's insistence on class conflict, contending that the northern agrarian system would provide opportunity for land ownership to every industrious white man. Unlike Marx, he assumed that these opportunities would last generations, precluding the proletarian future Marx foresaw. Marx asserted that the "whole labor of the world exists within that relation" with capital, something Lincoln explicitly denied. And he denied that northern workers suffered from the "wage slavery" Marx, American labor reformers, and pro-slavery advocates saw.

The world is agreed that labor is the source from which human wants are mainly supplied.... From this point, however, men immediately diverge. Much disputation is maintained as to the best way of applying and controlling the labor element. By some it is assumed that labor is available only in connection with capital—that nobody labors, unless somebody else, owning capital, somehow, by the use of that capital, induces him to do it. Having assumed this, they proceed to consider whether it is best that capital shall hire laborers, and thus induce them to work by their own consent; or buy them, and drive them to it without their consent. Having proceeded so far they naturally conclude that all laborers are necessarily either hired laborers, or slaves. They further assume that whoever is once a hired laborer, is fatally fixed in that condition for life; and thence again that his condition is as bad as, or worse than that of a slave. This is the "mud-sill" theory.

But another class of reasoners hold the opinion that there is no such relation between capital and labor...; and that there is no such thing as a freeman being fatally fixed for life, in the condition of a hired laborer . . . . They hold that labor is prior to, and independent of, capital; that, in fact, capital is the fruit of labor, and could never have existed if labor had not first existed—that labor can exist without capital, but that capital could never have existed without labor. Hence they hold that labor is the superior—greatly the superior—of capital.

They do not deny that there is, and probably always will be, a relation between labor and capital. The error, as they hold, is in assuming that the whole labor of the world exists within that relation. A few men own capital; and that few avoid labor themselves, and with their capital, hire, or buy, another few to labor for them. A large majority belong to neither class—neither work for others, nor have others working for them. Even in all our slave States, except South Carolina, a majority of the whole people of all colors, are neither slaves nor masters. In these Free States, a large majority are neither hirers or hired. Men, with their families—wives, sons and daughters—work for themselves, on their farms, in their houses and in their shops, taking the whole product to themselves, and asking no favors of capital on the one hand, nor of hirelings or slaves on the other . . . . The opponents of the "mud-sill" theory insist that there is not, of necessity, any such thing as the free hired laborer being fixed to that condition for life. There is demonstration for saying this. Many independent men, in this assembly, doubtless a few years ago were hired laborers. And their case is almost if not quite the general rule.

The prudent, penniless beginner in the world, labors for wages awhile, saves a surplus with which to buy tools or land, for himself; then labors on his own account another while, and at length hires another new beginner to help him. This, say its advocates, is free labor—the just and generous, and prosperous system, which opens the way for all—gives hope to all, and energy, and progress, and improvement of condition to all. If any continue through life in the condition of the hired laborer, it is not the fault of the system, but because of either a dependent nature which prefers it, or improvidence, folly, or singular misfortune . . . .

The old general rule was that educated people did not perform manual labor. They managed to eat their bread, leaving the toil of producing it to the uneducated. This was not an insupportable evil to the working bees, so long as the class of drones remained very small. But now, especially in these free States, nearly all are educated—quite too nearly all, to leave the labor of the uneducated, in any wise adequate to the support of the whole. It follows from this that henceforth educated people must labor. Otherwise, education itself would become a positive and intolerable evil. No country can sustain, in idleness, more than a small per centage of its numbers. The great majority must labor at something productive. From these premises the problem springs, "How can labor and education be the most satisfactory combined?"

By the "mud-sill" theory it is assumed that labor and education are incompatible.... According to that theory, a blind horse upon a treadmill, is a perfect illustration of what a laborer should be—all the better for being blind, that he could not tread out of place, or kick understandingly. According to that theory, the education of laborers, is not only useless, but pernicious, and dangerous. In fact, it is, in some sort, deemed a misfortune that laborers should have heads at all. Those same heads are regarded as explosive materials, only to be safely kept in damp places, as far as possible from that peculiar sort of fire which ignites them....

But Free Labor says "no!" Free Labor argues that, as the Author of man makes every individual with one head and one pair of hands, it was probably intended that heads and hands should cooperate as friends; and that that particular head, should direct and control that particular pair of hands. As each man has one mouth to be fed, and one pair of hands to furnish food, it was probably intended that that particular pair of hands should feed that particular mouth—that each head is the natural guardian, director, and protector of the hands and mouth inseparably connected with it; and that being so, every head should be cultivated, and improved, by whatever will add to its capacity for performing its charge. In one word Free Labor insists on universal education.

Cinncinnati German Workers to Lincoln, February 1861.

*German-Americans had hesitated to vote for Lincoln, fearing the nativism of some of his followers, but he ultimately received substantial support from them. German-American workers, allied with the communist-led International Association had made clear, in April 1858, their support for ethnic and racial equality; their fifth resolution read: "We recognize no distinction as to nationality or race, caste or status, color or sex; our goal is but reconciliation of all human interests, freedom and happiness for mankind, and the realization and unification of a world republic." In February 1861, Lincoln spoke before a group of Cincinnati German workers, perhaps including some allied with the International Association. The group promised to support his policies; they thought the election constituted a victory of free labor and "freedom over Slavery."*⁹

We, the German free workingmen of Cincinnati avail ourselves of this opportunity to assure you, our chosen chief magistrate, of our sincere and heartfelt regard. You earned our votes as the Champion of free labor and free homesteads.... We firmly adhere to the principles, which directed our votes in your favor. We trust, that you, the self-reliant because self-made man, will uphold the Constitution and the laws against secret treachery and avowed treason. If to this end you should be in need of men, the German free working men, with others, will rise as one man at your call, ready to risk their lives in the effort to maintain the victory already won by freedom over Slavery.

Lincoln's Speech to Germans, February 1861.

The Cincinnati Daily Commercial *report of Lincoln's February 1861 speech suggests that Lincoln wanted to assure these Germans, workers and businessmen alike, that his party welcomed them to the United States—necessary given the anti-Catholic and anti-immigrant posturing of the Know-Nothing Party, many of whose adherents became Republicans. At the same time, he championed a possible Homestead Act, one Congress passed and he signed about a year-and-a-half later. Note that he identified the "working class" with mechanics, that is, artisans, and not with the waged laborers Marx championed.*[10]

[W]orking men are the basis of all governments, for the plain reason that they are the most numerous, and as you added that those were the sentiments of the gentlemen present, representing not only the working class, but citizens of other callings than those of the mechanic, I am happy to concur with you in these sentiments, not only of the native born citizens, but also of the Germans and foreigners from other countries . . . .

In regard to the Homestead Law, I have to say that in so far as the Government lands can be disposed of, I am in favor of cutting up the wild lands into parcels, so that every poor man may have a home.

In regard to the Germans and foreigners, I esteem them no better than other people, nor any worse . . . . It is not my nature, when I see a people borne down by the weight of their shackles—the oppression of tyranny—to make their life more bitter by heaping upon them greater burdens; but rather would I do all in my power to raise the yoke, than to add anything that would tend to crush them. Inasmuch as our country is extensive and new, and the countries of Europe are densely populated, if there are any abroad who desire to make this the land of their adoption, it is not in my heart to throw aught in their way, to prevent them from coming to the United States.

Lincoln on the Homestead Act, 1863 Message to Congress.

In his December 8, 1863, annual message to Congress, Lincoln made clear his support for and success of the 1862 Homestead Act. Note that he considered the granting of free land to railroads as essential to the settlement of newly opened acreage.[11]

The quantity of land disposed of during the last and the first quarters of the present fiscal years was three million eight hundred and forty one thousand five hundred and forty nine acres, of which one hundred and sixty one thousand nine hundred and eleven acres were sold for cash, one million four hundred and fifty six thousand five hundred and fourteen acres were taken up under the homestead law, and the residue disposed of under laws granting lands for military bounties, for railroad and other purposes. It also appears that the sale of the public lands is largely on the increase.

It has long been a cherished opinion of some of our wisest statesmen that the people of the United States had a higher and more enduring interest in the early settlement and substantial cultivation of the public lands than in the amount of direct revenue to be derived from the sale of them. This opinion has had a controlling influence in shaping legislation upon the subject of our national domain. I may cite, as evidence of this, the liberal measures adopted in reference to actual settlers; the grant to the States of the overflowed lands within their limits in order to their being reclaimed and rendered fit for cultivation; the grants to railway companies of alternate sections of land upon the contemplated lines of their roads which, when completed, will so largely multiply the facilities for reaching our distant possessions. This policy has received its most signal and beneficent illustration in the recent enactment granting homesteads to actual settlers. Since the first day of January last the before-mentioned quantity of one million four hundred and fifty-six thousand five hundred and fourteen acres of land have been taken up under its provisions. This fact and the amount of sales furnish gratifying evidence of increasing settlement upon the public lands, notwithstanding the great struggle in which the energies of the nation have been engaged, and which has required so large a withdrawal of our citizens from their accustomed pursuits . . . .

MARX ON PROLETARIANS, CAPITALISTS, AND FREE LAND

Marx on the Homestead Act, August 1862.

In Die Presse, *Marx approvingly commented on the 1862 passage of the Homestead Act, whose premise he had ridiculed sixteen years earlier.*[12]

Apart from its financial legislation, [Congress] ... passed the Homestead Bill, which the Northern masses had long striven for in vain; in accordance with this Bill, part of the state lands is given gratis to the colonists, whether indigenous or new-comers, for cultivation.

Marx on farms and plantations, 1863.

Even at the time of the Civil War, Marx contended in his ongoing work on capitalism, colonial societies, like that of both North and South, had not yet become fully capitalist. Abundant land (for the time being), had in different ways, made it possible for farmers to attain an independent subsistence. In such farming colonies, Marx writes:[13]

[Farmers] are not capitalists, nor do they carry on capitalist production. They are more or less peasants who work themselves and whose main object ... is to produce their own livelihood, their means of subsistence.... They sell or exchange the excess of their products over their own consumption for imported manufactured commodities.... Even if capitalist production gradually comes into being, so that the sale of his products and the profit he makes from this sale become decisive for the farmer who himself works and owns his land; so long as, compared with capital and labour, land still exists in elemental abundance ..., the first type of colonisation will continue as well and production will therefore never be regulated according to the needs of the market.

Marx then contrasts such farms with slave plantations.

In ... plantations ... where ... production is intended for the world market ..., the slavery of Negroes precludes free wage-labour, which is the basis of capitalist production. But the business in which slaves are used is conducted by capitalists. The method of production which they introduce has not arisen out of slavery but is grafted on to it. In this case the same person is capitalist and landowner . . . . Neither does a class of farmers as distinct from landlords develop here.

Marx critiques Carey's views of land, 1869.

In 1869, in a letter to Frederick Engels, Marx critiqued the American political economist Henry Carey's arguments about American land use. Two years later, in an 1871 interview with the New York Herald, *he returned to his earlier position on "free" land, claiming that American land legislation sustained a land monopoly.*[14]

The factor that makes the interest on the capital invested in the land . . . part of differential rent is precisely the fact that the landowner receives this interest from capital which not he, but the tenant-farmer has invested in the land. This fact . . . is claimed [by Carey] to have no economic existence, because the tenant-farmer system has not yet developed in the United States. But this fact presents itself in another form there. The land jobber [land speculator, land seller] and not the tenant-farmer is ultimately paid in the price he gets for the land, for the capital expended by the tenant-farmer. Indeed, the history of the pioneers and the land jobbers in the United States is reminiscent of the worst horrors taking place, for instance, in Ireland.

Marx on workers and land monopoly, New York Herald *interview 1871.*

Correspondent: What are the principal aims of the society [the First Communist International] in the United States?
    Dr. Marx: To emancipate the workingman from the rule of politicians and to combat monopoly in all the many forms it is assuming there, especially that of the public lands. We want no more monstrous land grabs, no more grants to swindling railroad concerns, no more schemes for robbing the people of their birthright for the benefit of a few purse-proud monopolists.

CHAPTER 2

Slavery as a Social System

LINCOLN AND SLAVERY

Lincoln to Mary Speed, September 27, 1841.

Abraham Lincoln, already a lawyer and state legislator, first wrote about slavery in an 1841 letter to Mary Speed. Joshua Speed, her half-brother, had accompanied Lincoln on a steamboat to St. Louis. On that trip, Lincoln saw manacled slaves transported by their new master, from Kentucky, where he had purchased them, to his Deep South plantation. Similar horrors of the internal slave trade had already become staples of abolitionist writings. Like abolitionists, Lincoln understood that the planter had ruthlessly torn these unfortunate people from their families, but—unlike them—he lacked empathy, comparing them to "so many fish upon a trot-line." He expressed amazement that they appeared happy, playing the fiddle, singing, and joking. Social historians of slavery depict similar scenes as evidence of deep feeling, sadness, and resistance.[1]

... We got on board the Steam Boat Lebanon, in the locks of the Canal about 12. o'clock. M. of the day we left, and reached St. Louis the next Monday at 8 P.M. .... [A] fine example was presented on board the boat for contemplating the effect of condition upon human happiness. A gentleman had purchased twelve negroes in different parts of Kentucky and was taking them to a farm in the South. They were chained six and six together. A small iron clevis was around the left wrist of each, and this fastened to the main chain by a shorter one at a convenient distance from, the others; so that the negroes were strung together precisely like so many fish upon a trot-line.
In this condition they were being separated forever from the scenes of their childhood, their friends, their fathers and mothers, and brothers and sisters, and many of them, from their wives and children, and going into perpetual

slavery where the lash of the master is proverbially more ruthless and unrelenting than any other where; and yet amid all these distressing circumstances, as we would think them, they were the most cheerful and apparently happy creatures on board. One, whose offence for which he had been sold was an over-fondness for his wife, played the fiddle almost continually; and the others danced, sung, cracked jokes, and played various games with cards from day to day. How true it is that "God tempers the wind to the shorn lamb," or in other words, that He renders the worst of human conditions tolerable, while He permits the best, to be nothing better than tolerable . . . .

Lincoln to Joshua F. Speed, August 24, 1855.

Fourteen years later, in a letter to Joshua Speed, by then a Kentucky plantation owner, Lincoln recalled the trip as a scene that had tormented him and continued to do so. Espousing anti-slavery views, he reviewed the recent politics of slavery and tried to reconcile the constitutional rights slaveholders had with his abhorrence of slavery. Like other anti-slavery Whigs, he admitted these rights but sought to keep slavery out of new territories like Kansas.

The Missouri Compromise had prohibited slavery in territories located north of latitude 36°30' north, but the Kansas-Nebraska Act of 1854 had permitted voters in all territories to determine to allow or prohibit the institution. The Wilmot Proviso, named after its originator anti-slavery Congressman David Wilmot (D-PA), would have banned slavery from territories seized from Mexico in the Mexican-American War.

Lincoln's rhetoric demonstrates his political and ideological position on slavery. Northerners did "crucify their feelings" to support constitutional protections for slavery: he supported property rights but drew the line at "taking a negro to Kansas, to be held in slavery." His political position had become clear. No one who opposed slavery, as he did, could support "degrading classes of white people." He adhered to the Declaration of Independence and thought that the Know-Nothings (the American Party) would read Catholics and immigrants out of the Declaration's promise of equality as the country had long excluded "negroes." At the time of the letter, Lincoln still adhered to the Whig Party—he had not joined earlier anti-slavery parties, and he served his one term in the House of Representatives as a Whig.[2]

. . . You know I dislike slavery; and you fully admit the abstract wrong of it . . . . But you say that sooner than yield your legal right to the slave . . . , you would see the Union dissolved. I am not aware that any one is bidding you to yield that right; very certainly I am not . . . . I also acknowledge your rights and my obligations, under the constitution, in regard to your slaves. I confess I hate to see the poor creatures hunted down, and caught, and carried back to their stripes, and unrewarded toils; but I bite my lip and keep quiet. In 1841 you and I had together a tedious low-water trip, on a Steam Boat from Louisville to St. Louis. You may remember, as I well do, that from Louisville to the mouth of the Ohio there were, on board, ten or a dozen slaves, shackled together with irons. That sight was a continual torment to me; and I see something like it every time I touch the Ohio, or any other slave-border. It is hardly fair for you to assume, that I have no interest in a thing which has, and continually exercises, the power of making me miserable. You ought rather to appreciate how much the great body of the Northern people do crucify their feelings, in order to maintain their loyalty to the constitution and the Union.

I do oppose the extension of slavery, because my judgment and feelings so prompt me . . . In my humble sphere, I shall advocate the restoration of the Missouri Compromise, so long as Kansas remains a territory; and when, by all these foul means, it seeks to come into the Union as a Slave-state, I shall oppose it. I am very loth, in any case, to withhold my assent to the enjoyment of property acquired, or located, in good faith; but I do not admit that good faith, in taking a negro to Kansas, to be held in slavery, is a possibility with any man . . . . In my opposition to the admission of Kansas I shall have some company; but we may be beaten. If we are, I shall not, on that account, attempt to dissolve the Union . . . .

You say if Kansas fairly votes herself a free state, as a christian you will rather rejoice at it. All decent slave-holders talk that way; and I do not doubt their candor. But they never vote that way . . . . The slave-breeders and slave-traders, are a small, odious and detested class, among you; and yet in politics, they dictate the course of all of you, and are as completely your masters, as you are the masters of your own negroes . . . .

I am a whig; but others say there are no whigs, and that I am an abolitionist. When I was at Washington I voted for the Wilmot Proviso as good as forty times, and I never heard of any one attempting to unwhig me for that. I now do no more than oppose the extension of slavery. I am not a Know-Nothing . . . . How could I be? How can anyone who abhors the oppression of negroes, be in favor of degrading classes of white people? Our progress in degeneracy appears to me to be pretty rapid. As a nation, we began by declaring that "all men are created equal." We now practically read it "all men are created equal, except negroes." When the Know-Nothings get control, it will read "all men are created equal, except negroes, and foreigners, and catholics." When it comes to this I should prefer emigrating to some country where they make no pretence of loving liberty—to Russia, for instance, where despotism can be taken pure, and without the base alloy of hypocracy. . . .

MARX, SLAVERY, AND THE WORKING CLASS

Marx to Pavel Vasilyevich Annenkov, December 28, 1846.

Marx read about slavery in published works and articles written by his émigré friend Joseph Weydemeyer and occasionally wrote about the institution. His analytic tone contrasts sharply with Lincoln's moral outrage and political calculation. His thoughts about slavery are apparent in an 1847 letter about utopian socialist and anarchist Pierre-Joseph Proudhon's The Philosophy of Poverty, *an 1850 article, a letter to Engels, and in excerpts from the first volume of* Capital, *written during the Civil War.*

In 1847, Marx excoriated Proudhon's book for its lack of understanding of social relationships and economic change. Proudhon had misconstrued the division of labor, thinking it always remained the same, even as productive relations had changed greatly. Because he had failed to "see that economic categories are . . . abstraction of . . . [productive] relations," he had denied that man faced structural constraints and had to live within those "productive forces" in which he is born. Marx then interpreted Proudhon's comments on slavery as an example of his flawed method. Proudhon understood, like Marx, the relationship between slavery and modern industry. But he had made slavery a timeless, universal category. Marx presumes that Proudhon—like those southerners who insisted slavery was the best social relationship in every society—sees the need to speak only of the good, not the bad, side of slavery. In so doing, Marx relates slavery and freedom under capitalism, the slavery of America, and the supposed freedom of the "indirect slavery . . . of the proletariat." The "reflections on slavery" of this excerpt are Marx's summary of Proudhon's comments and should be read as damning criticism of Proundhon.[3]

Freedom and slavery constitute an antagonism. There is no need for me to speak either of the good or of the bad aspects of freedom. As for slavery, there is no need for me to speak of its bad aspects. The only thing requiring explanation is the good side of slavery. I do not mean indirect slavery, the slavery of proletariat; I mean direct slavery, the slavery of the Blacks in Surinam, in Brazil, in the southern regions of North America.

Direct slavery is as much the pivot upon which our present-day industrialism turns as are machinery, credit. Without slavery there would be no cotton, without cotton there would be no modern industry. It is slavery which has given value to the colonies, it is the colonies which have created world trade, and world trade is the necessary condition for large-scale machine industry. Consequently, prior to the slave trade, the colonies sent very few products to the Old World, and did not noticeably change the face of the world. Slavery is therefore an economic category of paramount importance. Without slavery, North America, the most progressive nation, would be transformed into a patriarchal country. Only wipe North America off the map and you will get anarchy, the complete decay of trade and modern civilisation. But to do away with slavery would be to wipe America off the map. Being an economic category, slavery has existed in all nations since the beginning of the world. All that modern nations have achieved is to disguise slavery at home and import it openly into the New World. After these reflections on slavery, what will the good Mr Proudhon do? He will seek the synthesis of liberty and slavery, the true golden mean, in other words the balance between slavery and liberty.

Marx and Engels, Neue Rheinische Zeitung Revue, 1850.[4]

The following article links American cotton production, 1848–1850, to English textile manufacturing, and sketches the links between slavery, the American cotton monopoly, and English capitalism. Weydemeyer had made similar arguments in essays Marx must have read. The short crop of 1850 had already led to diminished cloth production in England. By "English bourgeoisie," Marx meant the factory owners and other capitalists. Cotton production did expand to Egypt and other British colonies, but the United States retained its monopoly until the Confederacy switched from cotton to corn, reduced output of cotton to persuade European powers to recognize their independence, and the Union navy cut off some of the remaining Confederate supplies during the Civil War. Marx here, as other contemporary commentators in the United States and Europe, misconstrued North American slavery, for slaves produced rice, tobacco, and corn and could even be used, profitably, on small yeoman farms.

... [T]he English bourgeoisie has felt more forcefully than ever the power which the United States exercises over it, as a result of its hitherto unbroken monopoly of cotton production . . . . At the same time, that section of the English bourgeoisie kindly disposed towards the Negro has made the following discovery. "That the prosperity of Manchester is dependent on the treatment of slaves in Texas, Alabama and Louisiana is as curious as it is alarming." (*Economist*, 21 September 1850). That the decisive branch of English industry is based upon the existence of slavery in the southern states of the American union, that a Negro revolt in these areas could ruin the whole system of production as it exists today is, of course, an extremely depressing fact for the people who spent £20 million a few years ago on Negro emancipation in their own colonies. However, this fact leads to the only realistic solution of the slave question ... American cotton production is based on slavery. As soon as the industry ... cannot tolerate the United States' cotton monopoly any longer, cotton will be successfully mass-produced in other countries ... with free workers. But as soon as the free labour of other countries can deliver sufficient supplies of cotton to industry more cheaply than the slave labour of the United States, then American slavery will be broken together with the American cotton monopoly and the slaves will be emancipated, because they will have become useless as slaves ....

Marx to Engels, June 14, 1853.[5]

In an 1853 letter to Engels, Marx reported on his reading American political economist Henry Carey's Slavery at Home and Abroad, *a work that examined all forms of slavery and waged labor. Marx's negative judgment of the book mostly centers on Carey's critique of English industry, but he found Carey's analysis of slavery useful.*

Carey, the American political economist, has brought out a new book, *Slavery at Home and Abroad*. Here "slavery" covers all forms of servitude [and], wage-slavery .... The only thing of definite interest in the book is the comparison between Negro slavery as formerly practised by the English in Jamaica and elsewhere, and Negro slavery in the United States. He demonstrates how the main stock of Negroes in Jamaica always consisted of freshly imported barbarians, since their treatment by the English meant not only that the Negro population was not maintained, but also that ⅔ of the yearly imports always went to waste, whereas the present generation of Negroes in America is a native product, more or less Yankeefied, English speaking, etc., and hence *capable of being emancipated.*

THE SLAVE POWER AND NORTHERN SUPERIORITY

American victory in the Mexican-American War of 1846–1848 had increased the area of the United States by 900,000 square miles. Slavery advocates insisted that all American territories, including these lands be open to slavery; northern members of Congress wanted to retain the line between slave and free states the Compromise of 1820 created; anti-slavery politicians sought to prohibit slavery in territories. The armed conflict in Kansas, propelled by Senator Stephen Douglas's doctrine of Popular Sovereignty, which allowed citizens of territories to choose to form either a slave or free territory, led to intense political debate.

The map produced for John C. Fremont's 1856 Republican presidential campaign, illustrated two key points, ones Lincoln repeatedly made. "Reynolds's Political Map of the United States Designed to Exhibit the Comparative Area of the Free and Slave States, and the Territory Open to Slavery or Freedom by the Repeal of the Missouri Compromise" (see p. 37) depicts free states in red, slave states in black, and territories—now open by the Kansas-Nebraska Act (1854) to slavery—in green. The map shows the free states surrounded by the Slave Power, threatening to swallow up the entire nation. A small box, located under the New Mexico Territory, hammers home that point: "By the DEMOCRATIC(?) legislation of 1854, in repealing the Missouri Compromise, the institution of Slavery may be carried into ALL the Territories—the area of which is greater than that of all the States combined."

Anti-slavery politician John Jay asked readers to look at a similar map, a full-color engraving "blackened by slavery, and you will see that Kansas is the key to the large territory lying to the west of it, the boundless regions of Utah and New Mexico, extending hundreds of miles till they meet the eastern boundary of California. Is it not clear, that if we lose Kansas we shall in all probability lose not only the Indian Territory lying to the south of it, but these vast territories stretching to the westward, and large enough to make more than six States of the size of Pennsylvania?"[6] The map colored slave states black, free states red, and territories green. The map presented, in tabular form, statistical data from the 1850 US census, designed to show both the slave power and the superiority of free labor. One table, off the coast of the Carolinas, divided slaveholders into groups by number of slaves owned, documenting that a tiny number of men who pushed pro-slavery policies owned vast numbers of slaves. Tables at the bottom of the map showed the free states had greater population, higher property valuations, farm values, and capital in manufacturing; more newspapers with higher circulations and investment in education—but less territory—than the slave states and territories open to slavery.

LINCOLN AND THE POLITICS OF SLAVERY

Lincoln, 1854 Speech at Peoria.[7]

In innumerable speeches between 1854 and his inauguration, Lincoln addressed the pressing issues of slavery and slavery in the territories. He had less interest than Marx

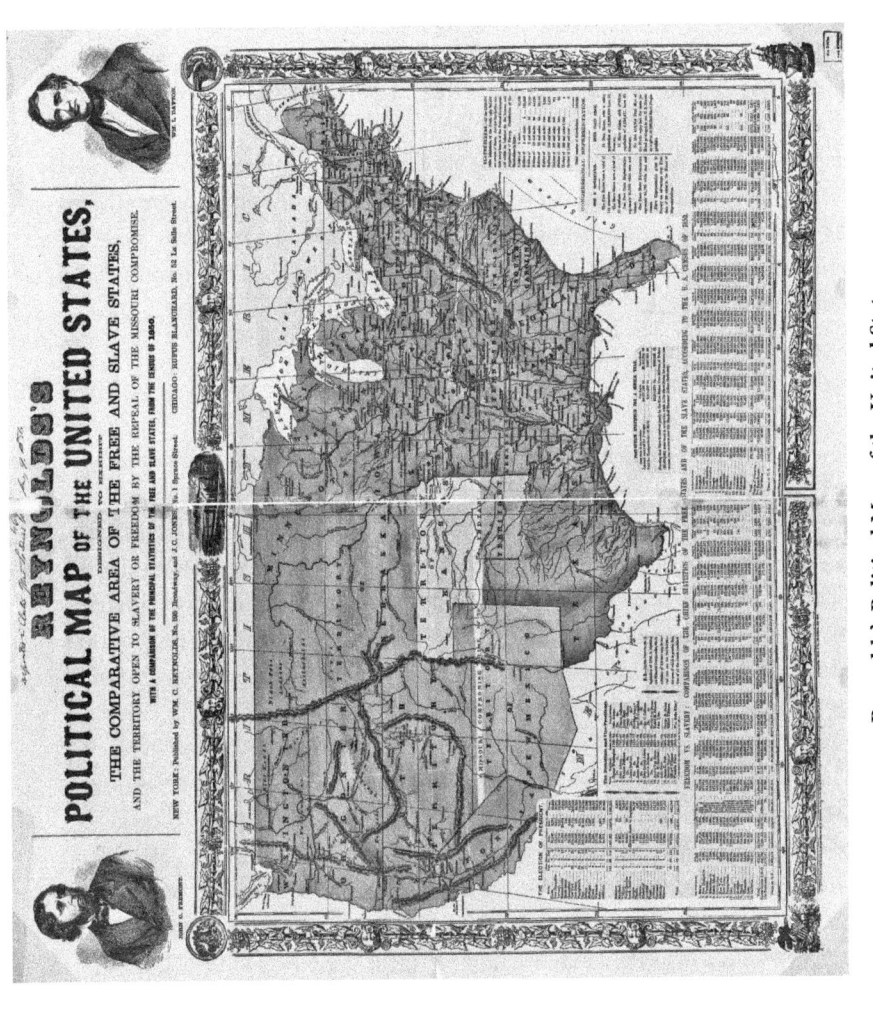

Reynolds's Political Map of the United States

in the role of slavery in the global economy. On October 16, 1854, at Peoria, Illinois, he gave a lengthy speech opposing the repeal of the Compromise of 1820. He opened the speech with a history of the Northwest Ordinance, which prohibited slavery in the Northwest Territories, the enforcement of the Missouri Compromise, the Wilmot Proviso (which, never passed, would have prohibited slavery in any territories gained from the war against Mexico), and the Compromise of 1850 (with its Fugitive Slave Law, the abolition of the slave trade in the District of Columbia, and the entrance of California as a free state). Lincoln struggled to find the best solution to the curse of slavery but found none—he would not free the slaves and send them to Liberia, for they would perish, nor would he admit to social equality between the races. Only very gradual emancipation might work.

Lincoln began by lambasting the end of the Compromise of 1820's prohibition of slavery in the northern territories and reprising the political history that led to its demise. He continued by analyzing the impact of allowing settlers to set up slave states in the territories and denied that Nebraska and Kansas were too far north to attract slaves, pointing to the slaves then toiling north of the Missouri compromise line.

... We even find some men, who drew their first breath, and every other breath of their lives, under this very restriction, now live in dread of absolute suffocation, if they should be restricted in the "sacred right" of taking slaves to Nebraska. That perfect liberty they sigh for—the liberty of making slaves of other people—Jefferson never thought of; their own father never thought of; they never thought of themselves, a year ago.... During this long period of time Nebraska had remained, substantially an uninhabited country, but now emigration to, and settlement within it began to take place.... The restriction of slavery by the Missouri Compromise directly applies to it.... On January 4th, 1854, Judge Douglas introduces a new bill to give Nebraska territorial government.... Before long the bill is so modified as to make two territories instead of one; calling the Southern one Kansas.... [I]t is so amended as to declare the Missouri Compromise inoperative and void; and, substantially, that the People who go and settle there may establish slavery, or exclude it, as they may see fit.... This is the repeal of the Missouri Compromise.... I think... that it is wrong; wrong in its direct effect, letting slavery into Kansas and Nebraska—and wrong in its prospective principle, allowing it to spread to every other part of the wide world, where men can be found inclined to take it.

This declared indifference, but... covert real zeal for the spread of slavery, I can not but hate. I hate it because of the monstrous injustice of slavery itself. I hate it because it deprives our republican example of its just influence in the world—enables the enemies of free institutions, with plausibility, to taunt us as hypocrites—causes the real friends of freedom to doubt our sincerity, and especially because it forces so many really good men amongst ourselves into an open war with the very fundamental principles of civil liberty—criticising the Declaration of Independence, and insisting that there is no right principle of action but self-interest . . . .

When southern people tell us they are no more responsible for the origin of slavery, than we; I acknowledge the fact. When it is said that . . . it is very difficult to get rid of it, in any satisfactory way, I can understand and appreciate the saying . . . . If all earthly power were given me . . . , [m]y first impulse would be to free all the slaves, and send them to Liberia,—to their own native land. But a moment's reflection would convince me, that whatever of high hope . . . , there may be in this, in the long run, its sudden execution is impossible. If they were all landed there in a day, they would all perish in the next ten days; and there are not surplus shipping and surplus money enough in the world to carry them there in many times ten days. What then? Free them all, and keep them among us as underlings? Is it quite certain that this betters their condition? I think I would not hold one in slavery, at any rate; yet the point is not clear enough for me to denounce people upon. What next? Free them, and make them politically and socially, our equals? My own feelings will not admit of this; and if mine would, we well know that those of the great mass of white people will not . . . . We can not, then, make them equals. It does seem to me that systems of gradual emancipation might be adopted; but for their tardiness in this, I will not undertake to judge our brethren of the south . . . .

But all this; to my judgment, furnishes no more excuse for permitting slavery to go into our own free territory, than it would for reviving the African slave trade by law. The law which forbids the bringing of slaves from Africa; and that which has so long forbid the taking them to Nebraska, can hardly be distinguished on any moral principle . . . .

It is argued that slavery will not go to Kansas and Nebraska, in any event. This is . . . a lullaby . . . . As to climate, a glance at the map shows that there are five slave States—Delaware, Maryland, Virginia, Kentucky, and Missouri—and also the District of Columbia, all north of the Missouri compromise line. The census returns of 1850 show that, within these, there are 867,276 slaves—being more than one-fourth of all the slaves in the nation. It is not climate, then, that will keep slavery out of these territories . . . .

Lincoln then turns to questions of race, slavery, and equality. If hogs and Negroes are the same, then no one could object to extending slavery to all the territories. But Negroes, he insists, are human—and Southerners, who signed on to punishing those who brought slaves from Africa, assumed as much. Self-government, he concludes, cannot allow some people to deny the humanity of others, as if they were wild beasts.

Equal justice to the south, it is said, requires us to consent to the extending of slavery to new countries. That is to say, inasmuch as you do not object to my taking my hog to Nebraska, therefore I must not object to you taking your slave. Now, I admit this is perfectly logical, if there is no difference between hogs and negroes. But while you thus require me to deny the humanity of the negro, I wish to ask whether you of the south yourselves, have ever been willing to do as much? . . . In 1820 you joined the north, almost unanimously, in declaring the African slave trade piracy, and in annexing to it the punishment of death. Why did you do this? If you did not feel that it was wrong, why did you join in providing that men should be hung for it? The practice was no more than bringing wild negroes from Africa, to sell to such as would buy them. But you never thought of hanging men for catching and selling wild horses, wild buffaloes or wild bears . . . .

The doctrine of self government is right . . . but it has no just application, as here attempted. Or perhaps I should rather say that whether it has such just application depends upon whether a negro is not or is a man. If he is not a man, why in that case, he who is a man may, as a matter of self-government, do just as he pleases with him. But if the negro is a man, is it not to that extent, a total destruction of self-government, to say that he too shall not govern himself? When the white man governs himself that is self-government; but when he governs himself, and also governs another man, that is more than self-government—that is despotism. If the negro is a man, why then my ancient faith teaches me that "all men are created equal;" and that there can be no moral right in connection with one man's making a slave of another . . . .

Whether slavery shall go into Nebraska, or other new territories, is not a matter of exclusive concern to the people who may go there. The whole nation is interested that the best use shall be made of these territories. We want them for the homes of free white people. This they cannot be, to any considerable extent, if slavery shall be planted within them. Slave States are places for poor white people to remove FROM; not to remove TO. New free States are the places for poor people to go to and better their condition. For this use, the nation needs these territories . . . .

Let no one be deceived. The spirit of seventy-six and the spirit of Nebraska, are utter antagonisms; and the former is being rapidly displaced by the latter. Fellow countrymen—Americans south, as well as north, shall we make no effort to arrest this? . . . Is there no danger to liberty itself, in discarding the earliest practice, and first precept of our ancient faith? In our greedy chase to make profit of the negro, let us beware, lest we "cancel and tear to pieces" even the white man's charter of freedom . . . .

The House Divided speech . . . .

Lincoln gave his "House Divided" speech just after receiving the 1858 Republican senatorial nomination.[8]

We are now far into the fifth year, since a policy was initiated, with the avowed object . . . of putting an end to slavery agitation. Under . . . that policy, that agitation has not only, not ceased, but has constantly augmented. In my opinion, it will not cease, until a crisis shall have been reached, and passed. "A house divided against itself cannot stand [Mark 3:25]" I believe this government cannot endure, permanently half slave and half free. I do not expect the Union to be dissolved—I do not expect the house to fall—but I do expect it will cease to be divided. It will become all one thing, or all the other. Either the opponents of slavery, will arrest the further spread of it, and place it where the public mind shall rest in the belief that it is in course of ultimate extinction; or its advocates will push it forward, till it shall become alike lawful in all the States, old as well as new—North as well as South.

Have we no tendency to the latter condition? Let any one who doubts, carefully contemplate that now almost complete legal combination . . . compounded of the Nebraska doctrine, and the Dred Scott decision . . . .
The new year of 1854 found slavery excluded from more than half the States by State Constitutions, and from most of the national territory by Congressional prohibition. Four days later, commenced the struggle, which ended in repealing that Congressional prohibition. This opened all the national territory to slavery . . . . This necessity had not been overlooked; but had been provided for, as well as might be, in the notable argument . . . called "sacred right of self government," which latter phrase, though expressive of the only rightful basis of any government, was so perverted in this attempted use of it as to amount to just this: That if any one man, choose to enslave another, no third man shall be allowed to object . . . . "But," said opposition members, ". . . let us amend the bill so as to expressly declare that the people of the territory may exclude slavery." "Not we," said the friends of the measure; and down they voted the amendment.

MARX AND THE OPENING OF THE CIVIL WAR

Marx to Engels, January 11, 1860.[9]

Marx followed events in the United States (as well as Britain and Europe) closely. As the Civil War drew closer, he occasionally commented on American slave politics. (He did not mention Lincoln until hostilities broke out.) In an early 1860 letter, he compared slave revolts in the United States, in particular the death of John Brown for leading the uprising at Harper's Ferry, Virginia, with agitation by Russian peasants against serfdom.

In my view, the most momentous thing happening in the world today is the slave movement—on the one hand, in America, started by the death of Brown, and in Russia, on the other . . . . Alexander has displeased the peasants, for the recent manifesto declares outright that, with emancipation, "the Communistic principle" must be abandoned. Thus, a "social" movement has been started both in the West and in the East. Together with the impending downbreak in Central Europe, this promises great things. I have just seen in the *Tribune* that there's been another slave revolt in Missouri which was put down, needless to say. But the signal has now been given. Should the affair grow serious by and by, what will become of Manchester?

Marx, "The North American Civil War," October 25, 1861.[10]

While the drama over the expansion of slavery and the election of Lincoln took place, Marx wrote little about slavery. But in an 1861 Die Presse article, Marx linked (inaccurately, since slavery prospered in the most northern reaches of the South) cotton to slavery and the economic (and political) need for slavery to expand.

The cultivation of the southern export articles, cotton, tobacco, sugar . . . , carried on by slaves, is only remunerative as long as it is conducted with large gangs of slaves, on a mass scale and on wide expanses of a naturally fertile soil, which requires only simple labour. Intensive cultivation, which depends less on fertility of the soil than on investment of capital, intelligence and energy of labour, is contrary to the nature of slavery. Hence the rapid transformation of states like Maryland and Virginia, which formerly employed slaves on the production of export articles, into states which raise slaves to export them into the deep South. Even in South Carolina, where the slaves form four-sevenths of the population, the cultivation of cotton has been almost completely stationary . . . due to the exhaustion of the soil . . . .

South Carolina has already been transformed in part into a slave-raising state, since it already sells slaves to the sum of four million dollars yearly to the states of the extreme South and South-west. As soon as this point is reached, the acquisition of new Territories becomes necessary, so that one section of the slaveholders with their slaves may occupy new fertile lands and that a new market for slave-raising, therefore for the sale of slaves, may be created . . . . [W]ithout the acquisition of Louisiana, Missouri and Arkansas by the United States, slavery in Virginia and Maryland would have been wiped out long ago. In the Secessionist Congress at Montgomery, Senator Toombs . . . strikingly formulated the economic law that commands the constant expansion of the territory of slavery. "In fifteen years," said he, "without a great increase in slave territory, either the slaves must be permitted to flee from the whites, or the whites must flee from the slaves . . . ."

Capital, *volume 1, 1867.*

In Capital, *volume 1, chapter 10, published in 1867 but written during the Civil War, Marx theorizes (somewhat inaccurately, given the tobacco and rice slaves had cultivated for export since the mid-seventeenth-century) that cotton led to the intensification of slavery, a reduction in slave life expectancy, and the breeding of slaves for sale (that is what he meant by "production of surplus labor itself," of slaves).*[11]

. . . . [A]s soon as people, whose production still moves within the lower forms of slave-labour . . . are drawn into the whirlpool of an international market dominated by the capitalistic mode of production, the sale of their products for export becoming their principal interest, the civilised horrors of over-work are grafted on the barbaric horrors of slavery . . . . Hence the negro labour in the Southern States of the American Union preserved something of a patriarchal character, so long as production was chiefly directed to immediate local consumption. But in proportion, as the export of cotton became of vital interest to these states, the over-working of the negro and sometimes the using up of his life in 7 years of labour became a factor in a calculated and calculating system. It was no longer a question of obtaining from him a certain quantity of useful products. It was now a question of production of surplus labour itself . . .

Marx returned to the impact of slavery and cotton in chapters 31, 15, and 7 of volume one of Capital, *where he also dealt with the ambiguities of machinery: English textile manufacturing, heavily machine dependent, led to further enslavement in the United States and to cotton cultivation that depended on slaves, rather than machines or even tools like plows. At the same time, it led to increased child labor in English factories (what Marx called "child-slavery").*[12]

Whilst the cotton industry introduced child-slavery in England, it gave in the United States a stimulus to the transformation of the earlier, more or less patriarchal slavery, into a system of commercial exploitation. In fact, the veiled slavery of the wage workers in Europe needed, for its pedestal, slavery pure and simple in the new world . . . .

Hence, as the use of machinery extends in a given industry, the immediate effect is to increase production in the other industries that furnish the first with means of production . . . . The number of the men condemned to work in coal and metal mines increased enormously owing to the progress of the English factory system; but during the last few decades this increase of number has been less rapid, owing to the use of new machinery in mining . . . . As to raw material, there is not the least doubt that the rapid strides of cotton spinning, not only pushed on with tropical luxuriance the growth of cotton in the United States, and with it the African slave trade, but also made the breeding of slaves the chief business of the border slave-states. When, in 1790, the first census of slaves was taken in the United States, their number was 697,000; in 1861 it had nearly reached four millions . . . .

The [slave] labourer here is . . . distinguishable only . . . from an animal as instrumentum semi-vocale [semi-vocal instrument], and from an implement as instrumentum mutum [silent instrument]. But he himself takes care to let both beast and implement feel that he is none of them, but is a man. He convinces himself with immense satisfaction, that he is a different being, by treating the one unmercifully and damaging the other . . . . Hence the principle, universally applied in this method of production, only to employ the rudest and heaviest implements and such as are difficult to damage owing to their sheer clumsiness. In the slave-states bordering on the Gulf of Mexico, down to the date of the civil war, ploughs constructed on old Chinese models, which turned up the soil like a hog or a mole, instead of making furrows, were alone to be found.

As Marx argued in Capital, *volume one, in savage selections from chapters 10 and 24, slave owners viewed slaves as commodities, much like livestock, and thus had a choice to use their profits for consumption or to buy more land or slaves.*[13]

The slave owner buys his labourer as he buys his horse. If he loses his slave, he loses capital, that can only be restored by new outlay in the slave-mart . . . .

The simple dictates of humanity therefore plainly enjoin the release of the capitalist from this martyrdom and temptation [of using money expropriated from laborers], in the same way that the Georgian slave-owner was lately delivered, by the abolition of slavery, from the painful dilemma, whether to squander the surplus-product, lashed out of his niggers [*sic*; written in English], entirely in champagne, or whether to reconvert a part of it into more niggers and more land.

In Capital, *volume 1, chapter 19, Marx compared the labor of free proletarians with that of slaves. Under slavery, the surplus workers produced accrued to the owners, who also suffered when productivity lagged; waged workers suffered (or perhaps advanced) by the labor power they sold. Until slavery ended, he wrote elsewhere, white laborers could neither achieve freedom nor successfully challenge their debased condition.*[14]

. . . [I]n the system of slavery . . . labour-power itself is sold. Only, in the slave system, the advantage of a labour-power above the average, and the disadvantage of a labour-power below the average, affects the slave-owner; in the wage-labour system, it affects the labourer himself, because his labour-power is, in the one case, sold by himself, in the other, by a third person.

CHAPTER 3

Secession and the Civil War
Lincoln, Secession, and the Border States

Southern fire-eaters had agitated for secession ever since the 1850 Nashville Convention. As soon as Lincoln was elected, they succeeded, and by the time he began his term, seven Deep South states had left the Union. Another four Upper South states left soon after the Union defense of Fort Sumter. Republican policies on enforcement of the Fugitive Slave Act and slavery in the territories stood behind their actions. They abandoned the Union because they feared that Lincoln would make states enforce the Fugitive Slave Act and succeed in prohibiting slavery from the territories; that would eliminate their ability to prevent the Senate from passing anti-slavery legislation, rendering their slave property insecure.

Before he took office, Lincoln struggled to keep the border slave states—Maryland, Delaware, Kentucky, and Missouri—in the Union, while insisting on ending slavery in the territories. A month after the election, he wrote notes to Illinois Senator Lyman Trumbull and Illinois Congressman William Kellogg, suggesting the limits of his willingness to compromise: he supported enforcement of the Fugitive Slave Act but not slavery in the territories much less Senator Stephen Douglas's doctrine of Popular Sovereignty, one that would allow territories to vote on slavery or freedom. That would lead to violence as Southerners made all the Southwest into slave states. A fuller statement came in a mid-December letter to New York politician and newspaper editor Thurlow Weed, responding to Weed's idea of convening a convocation of governors to seek compromise.[1]

Lincoln to Lyman Turnbull, December, 1860.

Let there be no compromise on the question of *extending* slavery. If there be, all our labor is lost, and, ere long, must be done again. The dangerous ground—that into which some of our friends have a hankering to run—is

Pop. Sov. Have none of it. Stand firm. The tug has to come, & better now, than any time hereafter.

Lincoln to William Kellogg, December, 1860.

Entertain no proposition for a compromise in regard to the extension of slavery. The instant you do, they have us under again; all our labor is lost, and sooner or later must be done over. Douglas is sure to be again trying to bring in his "Pop. Sov." Have none of it. The tug has to come & better now than later. You know I think the fugitive slave clause of the constitution ought to be enforced—to put it on the mildest form, ought not to be resisted.

Lincoln to Thurlow Weed, December, 1860.

Should the convocation of Governors . . . seem desirous to know my views . . . , tell them you judge from my speeches that I will be inflexible on the territorial question; that I probably think either the Missouri line extended, or Douglas' and Eli Thayer's Pop. Sov. would lose us every thing we gained by the election; that filibustering [military invasions] for all South of us, and making slave states of it, would follow in spite of us, under either plan. Also, that I probably think all opposition, real and apparant, to the fugitive slave [clause] of the constitution ought to be withdrawn. I believe you can pretend to find but little, if anything, in my speeches, about secession; but my opinion is that no state can, in any way lawfully, get out of the Union, without the consent of the others; and that it is the duty of the President, and other government functionaries to run the machine as it is.

Green to Buchanan, December 28, 1860.

Later in December, Lincoln saw long-time friend and former newspaper editor Duff Green, who had been sent to Springfield to discuss congressional negotiations on compromise and to urge Lincoln to come to Washington to lobby Republicans to support pro-slavery constitutional amendments. These Crittenden resolutions kept slavery open in nearly all the territories captured in the Mexican War, required payment for the value of successful runaway slaves, and prohibited any constitutional amendment outlawing slavery in perpetuity. Lincoln would not support such resolutions, ones that eviscerated Republican

Party insistence that mandated the end of slavery in the territories. Green, who did want to avoid the break-up of the Union, harangued Lincoln with pro-slavery arguments (what Lincoln called "slavery 'propagandism'") and answered every anti-slavery answer Lincoln gave. After that discussion, he wrote President James Buchanan about his discussions and later reported his side of the discussion in the New York Herald.²

> I have had a long conversation with Mr. Lincoln. I brought with me a copy of the resolutions submitted by Mr. Crittenden which he read over several times and said that he believed that the adoption of the line proposed would quiet for the present, the agitation of the slavery question, but believed it would be renewed by the seizure and attempted annexation of Mexico. He said that the real question at issue between the North and the South was slavery "propagandism" and that upon that issue the Republican party was opposed to the South, and that he was with his own party; that he had been elected by that party, and intended to sustain his party in good faith; but added, that the question on the amendments to the Constitution and the questions submitted by Mr. Crittenden belonged to the people and States in legislatures or conventions, and that he would be inclined not only to acquiesce, but to give full force and effect to their will thus expressed. Seeing that he was embarrassed by his sense of duty to his party, I suggested that he might so frame a letter to me as to refer the measures for the preservation of the Union to the action of the people in the several States, and he promised to prepare a letter . . . .

Lincoln to Green, December 28, 1860.

Ideological blinders prevented Green from seeing that Lincoln disagreed with his program and would not lobby Republicans to accept it. At the end of December, Lincoln sent the missive to Senator Trumbull, who probably gave it to Green. Lincoln denied interest in amending the Constitution to protect slavery from congressional interference but supported the rights of states to sustain slavery (their "domestic institutions"). Amendments were stuck in a congressional committee and would not reach the floor unless Republicans voted for them, which they would not do without Lincoln's support. He would allow his letter to be published only if half the senators from six seceding states signed a statement renouncing secession, something he knew they would reject.³

> I do not desire any amendment of the Constitution. Recognizing, however, that questions of such amendment rightfully belong to the American People, I should not feel justified, nor inclined, to withhold from them, if I could,

a fair opportunity of expressing their will thereon, through either of the modes prescribed in the instrument.

In addition I declare that the maintenance inviolate of the rights of the States, and especially the right of each state to order and control its own domestic institutions according to its own judgment exclusively, is essential to that balance of powers on which the perfection, and endurance of our political fabric depends—and I denounce the lawless invasion, by armed force, of the soil of any State or Territory, no matter under what pretext, as the gravest of crimes.

I am greatly averse to writing anything for the public at this time; and I consent to the publication of this, only upon the condition that six of the twelve United States Senators for the States of Georgia, Alabama, Mississippi, Louisiana, Florida, and Texas shall sign their names to what is written on this sheet below my name, and allow the whole to be published together.

[*The statement Lincoln wanted the senators to sign:*] We recommend to the people of the States we represent respectively, to suspend all action for dismemberment of the Union, at least, until some act, deemed to be violative of our rights, shall be done by the incoming administration.

When he saw the letter, Green knew Lincoln had rejected his suggestions. On January 7, 1861, he wrote Lincoln, regretting his suggestion and announcing the publication of the interview:[4]

I regret your unwillingness to recommend an amendment to the Constitution which would arrest the progress of the Secession. The fact of my having been to Springfield having been published I have deemed it expedient to publish a statement which will probably appear in the N.Y. Herald of tomorrow.

First Inaugural Address.[5]

Lincoln expanded on these themes in his First Inaugural Address. By sidestepping the issue of slavery, Lincoln pretended that the war only concerned the preservation of the Union. He assured slaveholders that his administration would enforce the Fugitive Slave Act and would not challenge slavery where it currently existed. Nor would he go to war, unless the Confederacy attacked federal property. Such a strategy may have been essential to keep the Border States in the Union, but it led British conservatives to urge support for the Confederacy. At the same time, it fooled no one in the United States—abolitionists knew a war, if it broke out, would be about slavery, and the fire-eaters knew they left the Union because of the policies on slavery the new administration would follow.

Apprehension seems to exist among the people of the Southern States, that by the accession of a Republican Administration, their property, and their peace, and personal security, are to be endangered. There has never been any reasonable cause for such apprehension.... I do but quote from one of [my]... speeches when I declare that "I have no purpose, directly or indirectly, to interfere with the institution of slavery in the States where it exists. I believe I have no lawful right to do so, and I have no inclination to do so." Those who nominated and elected me did so with full knowledge that I had made this, and many similar declarations, and had never recanted them.... I now reiterate these sentiments...: that the property, peace and security of no section are to be in anywise endangered by the now incoming Administration. I add too, that all the protection which, consistently with the Constitution and the laws, can be given, will be cheerfully given to all the States when lawfully demanded, for whatever cause....

There is much controversy about the delivering up of fugitives from service or labor. The clause I now read is as plainly written in the Constitution as any other of its provisions: "No person held to service or labor in one State, under the laws thereof, escaping into another, shall, in consequence of any law or regulation therein, be discharged from such service or labor, but shall be delivered up on claim of the party to whom such service or labor may be due." It is scarcely questioned that this provision was intended by those who made it, for the reclaiming of what we call fugitive slaves.... All members of Congress swear their support to the whole Constitution.... To the proposition, then, that slaves whose cases come within the terms of this clause, "shall be delivered up," their oaths are unanimous....

It is seventy-two years since the first inauguration of a President under our national Constitution. During that period fifteen different and greatly distinguished citizens, have, in succession, administered the executive branch of the government. They have conducted it through many perils; and, generally, with great success. Yet... I now enter upon the same task..., under great and peculiar difficulty. A disruption of the Federal Union heretofore only menaced, is now formidably attempted.

Speaking to citizens of the seceding states, he deemed the Union perpetual and those who formed new governments rebels or revolutionaries. He insisted that no government would permit its own destruction through secession. The North had never broken any constitutional guarantees to southern slaveholders, and only such behavior might warrant rebellion. The Union was worth preserving, not only because of these constitutional guarantees but also because of "[t]he mystic chords of memory, stretching from every battle-field, and patriot grave, to every living heart and hearthstone, all over this broad land."

I hold, that in contemplation of universal law, and of the Constitution, the Union of these States is perpetual.... [N]o government proper, ever had a provision in its organic law for its own termination. Continue to execute all the express provisions of our national Constitution, and the Union will endure forever—it being impossible to destroy it, except by some action not provided for in the instrument itself.... But if destruction of the Union, by one, or by a part only, of the States, be lawfully possible, the Union is less perfect than before the Constitution, having lost the vital element of perpetuity. It follows from these views that no State, upon its own mere motion, can lawfully get out of the Union,—that resolves and ordinances to that effect are legally void; and that acts of violence, within any State or States, against the authority of the United States, are insurrectionary or revolutionary....

I therefore consider that, in view of the Constitution and the laws, the Union is unbroken; and, to the extent of my ability, I shall take care, as the Constitution itself expressly enjoins upon me, that the laws of the Union be faithfully executed in all the States. Doing this I deem to be only a simple duty on my part; and I shall perform it, so far as practicable, unless my rightful masters, the American people, shall withhold the requisite means, or, in some authoritative manner, direct the contrary.... In doing this there needs to be no bloodshed or violence; and there shall be none, unless it be forced upon the national authority. The power confided to me, will be used to hold, occupy, and possess the property, and places belonging to the government, and to collect the duties and imposts; but beyond what may be necessary for these objects, there will be no invasion....

... All profess to be content in the Union, if all constitutional rights can be maintained. Is it true, then, that any right, plainly written in the Constitution, has been denied? I think not.... Think, if you can, of a single instance in which a plainly written provision of the Constitution has ever been denied. If, by the mere force of numbers, a majority should deprive a minority of any clearly written constitutional right, it might, in a moral point of view, justify revolution—certainly would, if such right were a vital one. But such is not our case. All the vital rights of minorities, and of individuals, are so plainly assured to them, by affirmations and negations, guaranties and prohibitions, in the Constitution, that controversies never arise concerning them. But no organic law can ever be framed with a provision specifically applicable to every question which may occur in practical administration.... May Congress prohibit slavery in the territories? The Constitution does not expressly say. Must Congress protect slavery in the territories? The Constitution does not expressly say.

From questions of this class spring all our constitutional controversies, and we divide upon them into majorities and minorities. If the minority will not acquiesce, the majority must, or the government must cease.... If a minority, in such case, will secede rather than acquiesce, they make a precedent which, in turn, will divide and ruin them; for a minority of their own will secede from them, whenever a majority refuses to be controlled by such minority. For instance, why may not any portion of a new confederacy, a year or two hence, arbitrarily secede again, precisely as portions of the present Union now claim to secede from it....

Plainly, the central idea of secession, is the essence of anarchy. A majority, held in restraint by constitutional checks, and limitations, and always changing easily, with deliberate changes of popular opinions and sentiments, is the only true sovereign of a free people. Whoever rejects it, does, of necessity, fly to anarchy or to despotism. Unanimity is impossible; the rule of a minority, as a permanent arrangement, is wholly inadmissable; so that, rejecting the majority principle, anarchy, or despotism in some form, is all that is left....

One section of our country believes slavery is right, and ought to be extended, while the other believes it is wrong, and ought not to be extended. This is the only substantial dispute. The fugitive slave clause of the Constitution, and the law for the suppression of the foreign slave trade, are each as well enforced.... The great body of the people abide by the dry legal obligation in both cases, and a few break over in each. This... cannot be perfectly cured; and it would be worse in both cases after the separation of the sections, than before. The foreign slave trade, now imperfectly suppressed, would be ultimately revived without restriction, in one section; while fugitive slaves, now only partially surrendered, would not be surrendered at all, by the other....

This country, with its institutions, belongs to the people who inhabit it. Whenever they shall grow weary of the existing government, they can exercise their constitutional right of amending it, or their revolutionary right to dismember, or overthrow it. I can not be ignorant of the fact that many worthy, and patriotic citizens are desirous of having the national constitution amended. While I make no recommendation of amendments, I fully recognize the rightful authority of the people over the whole subject, to be exercised in either of the modes prescribed in the instrument itself; and I should, under existing circumstances, favor, rather than oppose, a fair opportunity being afforded the people to act upon it . . . .

In your hands, my dissatisfied fellow countrymen, and not in mine, is the momentous issue of civil war. The government will not assail you. You can have no conflict, without being yourselves the aggressors. You have no oath registered in Heaven to destroy the government, while I shall have the most solemn one to "preserve, protect and defend" it . . . . We are not enemies, but friends. We must not be enemies. Though passion may have strained, it must not break our bonds of affection. The mystic chords of memory, stretching from every battle-field, and patriot grave, to every living heart and hearthstone, all over this broad land, will yet swell the chorus of the Union, when again touched, as surely they will be, by the better angels of our nature.

MARX ON SECESSION AND THE START OF WAR

Marx to Engels, July 5, 1861.[6]

Conservative European leaders took Lincoln at his word: if the war was a civil war, one unrelated to slavery, then the doctrine of national self-determination should hold sway and the Union should, by implication, allow the South to go in peace; at best, they would stay neutral, recognizing the Confederates as combatants, and not establish diplomatic relations with them. Marx, who closely followed events in the United States, from the time of Lincoln's election and who knew the country's political history, had a different view. He had followed the succession conventions and knew the conflicted political geography of the South, one which divided coastal areas from the mountains. Marx wrote Engels on June 19, 1861, that "from the facts appearing in the Tribune *I see that the North is now speaking openly of a slave war and the abolition of slavery." Writing to Engels about succession in July 1861, he argued that a conspiracy of large slaveholders fomented succession, supporting his argument by quotes from two Unionist southern planters and southern newspapers, calling the succession conventions "mere mockery," secret meetings, undemocratic, deceptive, and opposed by the common people.*

As to the secession business, the matter has been quite wrongly represented in the English papers. Everywhere, with the exception of *South Carolina*, there was the strongest opposition to secession.... *Delaware* refused even to call a convention for this purpose. *Tennessee* ditto. Its Democratic Legislature took it out of the Union by coup de main. Admittedly, an election was later held to ratify this invalid Act. This took place under a reign of terrorism. More than ⅓ didn't vote at all. Of the remainder, ⅓ were against secession, including the whole of East Tennessee, which at this moment is arming to oppose the secessionists....

Virginia. The people elected a Union Convention (by a majority). Some of these chaps allowed themselves to be bought. When the Southern fever was at its height—fall of Sumter—an Ordinance of Secession was passed secretly by 88 to 55. All other moves—while the Ordinance continued to be kept secret—aimed at the capture of the Federal Navy Yard at Norfolk and the Federal Armory at Harper's Ferry were carried out secretly. Were betrayed to the Federal Authorities before their execution....

Gulf States. A popular vote proper was taken only in a few states. In most of them, the conventions, which were chosen to decide the attitude of the southern states to Lincoln's election ... usurped the power not only to decide on secession but also to recognise the Constitution.... The interests of the mountain districts, the west of Carolina, the east of Tennessee, the north of Alabama and Georgia, are very different from those of the southern swamps....

Marx, "The American Question in England."[7]

Marx first wrote extensively about the causes of the Civil War in an October 11, 1861, article in New York Daily Tribune *attacking the pro-Confederacy sympathies of English newspapers. He insisted slavery led to war, even if the Union did not aim to abolish slavery. The South, after all, had started the war and made clear it did so only to defend slavery. At the outset, he referred to a letter Harriet Beecher Stowe published in two English newspapers in which she defended the Union, writing that northern abolitionists "consider this war is a great Anti-Slavery War, not in form, but in fact: not in proclamation, but in the intense conviction and purpose of each of the contending parties, and still more in the inevitable overruling indications of divine Providence."*[8]

Mrs. Beecher Stowe's letter to Lord Shaftesbury ... has done a great deal of good, by forcing the anti-Northern organs of the London press to speak out and lay before the general public the ostensible reasons for their hostile tone against the North, and their ill-concealed sympathies with the South, which looks rather strange on the part of people affecting an utter horror of Slavery. Their first and main grievance is that the present American war is "not one for the abolition of Slavery," and that, therefore, the high-minded Britisher, used to undertake wars of his own, and interest himself in other people's wars only on the basis of "broad humanitarian principles," cannot be expected to feel any sympathy with his Northern cousins.

"In the first place" says *The Economist*, "the assumption that the quarrel between the North and South is a quarrel between Negro freedom on the one side and Negro Slavery on the other, is as impudent as it is untrue." "The North," says *The Saturday Review*, "does not proclaim abolition, and never pretended to fight for Anti-Slavery. The North has not hoisted . . . the sacred symbol of justice to the Negro; its cri de guerre is not unconditional abolition." . . .

Now . . . the premiss [sic] must be conceded. The war has not been undertaken . . . to put down Slavery, and the United States authorities themselves have taken the greatest pains to protest against any such idea. But then, it ought to be remembered that it was not the North, but the South, which undertook this war; the former acting only on the defense. If . . . the North, after long hesitations, and an exhibition of forbearance unknown in . . . European history, drew at last the sword, not for crushing Slavery, but for saving the Union, the South, on its part, inaugurated the war by loudly proclaiming "the peculiar institution" as the only and main end of the rebellion. It confessed to fight for the liberty of enslaving other people, a liberty which, despite the Northern protests, it asserted to be put in danger by the victory of the Republican party and the election of Mr. Lincoln . . . . The Confederate Congress boasted that its new-fangled constitution, as distinguished from the Constitution of the Washingtons, Jeffersons, and Adams's, had recognized for the first time Slavery as a thing good in itself, a bulwark of civilization, and a divine institution. If the North professed to fight but for the Union, the South gloried in rebellion for the supremacy of Slavery. If Anti-Slavery and idealistic England felt not attracted by the profession of the North, how came it to pass that it was not violently repulsed by the cynical confessions of the South?

The Saturday Review helps itself out of this ugly dilemma by disbelieving the declarations of the seceders themselves. It sees deeper than this, and discovers "that Slavery had very little to do with Secession;" the declarations of Jeff. Davis and company . . . being mere "conventionalisms" with "about as much meaning as the conventionalisms about violated altars and desecrated hearths, which always occur in such proclamations." . . .

One might suppose that [the] . . . oracles of public opinion in England had made themselves sufficiently familiar with the contemporaneous history to not need Mrs. Stowe's information . . . . The progressive abuse of the Union by the slave power, working through its alliance with the Northern Democratic party is . . . the general formula of the United States history since the beginning of this century. The successive compromise measures mark the successive degrees of the encroachment by which the Union became more and more transformed into the slave of the slave-owner . . . . If the positive and final result of each single contest told in favor of the South, the attentive observer of history could not but see that every new advance of the slave power was a step forward to its ultimate defeat . . . . The encroachments of the slaveholding power reached their maximum point, when, by the Kansas-Nebraska bill, for the first time . . . every legal barrier to the diffusion of Slavery within the United States territories was broken down, . . . when, later on, by the Dred Scott decision, diffusion of Slavery by the Federal power was proclaimed as the law of the American Constitution . . . . But, concurrently with this climax of Southern encroachments, carried by the connivance of the Northern Democratic party, there were unmistakable signs of Northern antagonistic agencies having gathered such strength as must soon turn the balance of power. The Kansas war, the formation of the Republican party, and the large vote cast for Mr. Frémont during the Presidential election of 1856, were so many palpable proofs that the North had accumulated sufficient energies to rectify the aberrations which United States history, under the slave owners' pressure, had undergone, for half a century, and to . . . return to the true principles of its development . . . .

He went on to attack London newspapers for lambasting the Union because it did not go to war to abolish slavery—while still supporting a slave republic. In so doing, the English political establishment judged the pro-slavery action of some Northerners more harshly than those of men who owned slaves. The English charged, Marx concluded, that Northerners had the temerity to merely oppose the expansion of slavery into the territories, something those in both regions knew would ultimately destroy the institution.

Is it the fault of the American North that the English pressmen were taken quite unawares by the violent clash of the antagonistic forces, the friction of which was the moving power of its history for half a century? . . . Instead of answering . . . *The Economist* exclaims: "Can we forget [. . .] that

Abolitionists have habitually been as ferociously persecuted and maltreated in the North and West as in the South? Can it be denied that the testiness and half-heartedness, not to say insincerity, of the Government at Washington, have for years supplied the chief impediment which has thwarted our efforts for the effectual suppression of the slave trade on the coast of Africa; while a vast proportion of the clippers actually engaged in that trade have been built with Northern capital, owned by Northern merchants and manned by Northern seamen?"

This is, in fact, a masterly piece of logic. Anti-Slavery England cannot sympathize with the North breaking down the withering influence of slaveocracy, because she cannot forget that the North, while bound by that influence, supported the slave-trade, mobbed the Abolitionists, and had its Democratic institutions tainted by the slavedriver's prejudices.... She must needs sullenly cavil at the present movement of the Northern resurrection, cheer up the Northern sympathizers with the slave-trade, branded in the Republican platform, and coquet with the Southern slaveocracy, setting up an empire of its own, because she cannot forget that the North of yesterday was not the North of to-day....

Still there is one concession made by the anti-Northern English press. The *Saturday* snob tells us: "What was at issue in Lincoln's election, and what has precipitated the convulsion, was merely the limitation of the institution of Slavery to States where that institution already exists." And *The Economist* remarks: "It is true enough that it was the aim of the Republican party which elected Mr. Lincoln to prevent Slavery from spreading into the unsettled Territories.... It may be true that the success of the North, if complete and unconditional, would enable them to confine Slavery within the fifteen States which have already adopted it, and might thus lead to its eventual extinction—though this is rather probable than certain...."

The limitation of Slavery to its constitutional area, as proclaimed by the Republicans, was the distinct ground upon which the menace of Secession was first uttered in the House of Representatives on December 19, 1859. Mr. Singleton (Mississippi) having asked Mr. Curtis (Iowa), "if the Republican party would never let the South have another foot of slave territory while it remained in the Union," and Mr. Curtis having responded in the affirmative, Mr. Singleton said this would dissolve the Union. His advice to Mississippi was the sooner it got out of the Union the better.... Quite apart from the economical law which makes the diffusion of Slavery a vital condition for its maintenance within its constitutional areas, the leaders of the South had never deceived themselves as to its necessity for keeping up their political sway over the United States.... Moreover, the Oligarchy of the 300,000 slave-owners could not even maintain their sway at home save by constantly throwing out to their white plebeians the bait of prospective conquests within and without the frontiers of the United States. If, then, according to the oracles of the English press, the North had arrived at the fixed resolution of circumscribing Slavery within its present limits, and of thus extinguishing it in a constitutional way, was this not sufficient to enlist the sympathies of Anti-Slavery England?

But the English Puritans seem indeed not to be contented save by an explicit Abolitionist war. "This," says *The Economist* "therefore, not being a war for the emancipation of the Negro race, [. . .] on what other ground can we be fairly called upon to sympathize so warmly with the Federal cause?" "There was a time," says *The Examiner*, "when our sympathies were with the North, thinking that it was really in earnest in making a stand against the encroachments of the Slave States," and in adopting "emancipation as a measure of justice to the black race." However, in the very same numbers in which these papers tell us that they cannot sympathize with the North because its war is no Abolitionist war, we are informed that "the desperate expedient of proclaiming Negro emancipation and summoning the slaves to a general insurrection," is a thing "the mere conception of which [. . .] is repulsive and dreadful . . . " Thus the English eagerness for the Abolitionist war is all cant . . . .

Marx, "The North American Civil War."⁹

Marx had no need to detail the politics of slavery and abolition for the anti-slavery readers of the New-York Tribune. *But he had to do so for his October 25, 1861, report to the Vienna paper* Die Presse. *He extended the arguments made in the* Tribune *and explored the history of the slavery controversy in the coming of the Civil War. Toward the end of this selection, he referred to Confederate Vice President Alexander Stephens's pro-slavery "Cornerstone Speech," in which Stephens insisted that the "corner-stone" of the new Confederate government "rests upon the great truth, that the negro is not equal to the white man; that slavery—subordination to the superior race, is his natural and normal condition. This, our new government, is the first, in the history of the world, based upon this great physical, philosophical, and moral truth."*¹⁰

For months the leading weekly and daily papers of the London press have been reiterating the same litany on the American Civil War. While they insult the free states of the North, they anxiously defend themselves against the suspicion of sympathising with the slave states . . . . In essence the extenuating arguments read: The war between the North and South is a tariff war. The war is, further, not for any principle, does not touch the question of slavery and in fact turns on Northern lust for sovereignty. Finally, even if justice is on the side of the North, does it not remain a vain endeavour to want to subjugate eight million Anglo-Saxons by force! Would not separation of the South release the North from all connection with Negro slavery and ensure for it, with its twenty million inhabitants and its vast territory, a higher, hitherto scarcely dreamt-of, development? Accordingly, must not the North welcome secession as a happy event, instead of wanting to overrule it by a bloody and futile civil war . . . ?

[T]he war did not originate with the North, but with the South . . . . For months the secessionists appropriated the Union's forts, arsenals, shipyards, customs houses, pay offices, ships and supplies of arms, insulted its flag and took prisoner bodies of its troops. Finally the secessionists resolved to force the Union government out of its passive attitude by a blatant act of war, and solely for this reason proceeded to the bombardment of Fort Sumter . . . . News of this had hardly been telegraphed to Montgomery, the seat of the Secession Congress, when War Minister Walker . . . prophesied that before the first of May the flag of the Southern Confederacy will wave from the dome of the old Capitol in Washington and within a short time perhaps also from the Faneuil Hall in Boston. Only now ensued the proclamation in which Lincoln called for 75,000 men to defend the Union . . . .

The question of the principle of the American Civil War is answered by . . . Stephens, the Vice-President of the Southern Confederacy, [who] declared in the Secession Congress that what essentially distinguished the Constitution newly hatched at Montgomery from the Constitution of Washington and Jefferson was that now for the first time slavery was recognised as an institution good in itself, and as the foundation of the whole state edifice, whereas the revolutionary fathers, men steeped in the prejudices of the eighteenth century, had treated slavery as an evil imported from England and to be eliminated in the course of time . . . . If, therefore, it was indeed only in defence of the Union that the North drew the sword, had not the South already declared that the continuance of slavery was no longer compatible with the continuance of the Union . . . ?

To show the significance of slavery in the upcoming war, Marx reviewed the history of the slavery issue, emphasizing the Buchanan administration's enforcement of the Fugitive Slave Act, the pro-slavery Kansas Nebraska Act, and the Dred Scott case. Secession occurred after the Democratic Party split in 1860, which led to Lincoln's election as president, making it difficult to impose slavery on new territories, followed by the succession of South Carolina, Georgia, and Mississippi. He then turned to the impact of slaveholders on foreign policy, insisting that the federal government, under Buchanan, supported the reopening of the Atlantic slave trade, and that some fifteen thousand were actually imported, a highly inflated figure. A "turning point" at last came: the civil war in Kansas, sustained by southern "border rabble," that led to the formation of the Republican Party.

Given the much greater population of the free states and the fear of poor southern whites, southern slaveholders needed to create new slave states to protect their control of the US Senate and thus to preserve slavery. By the North-West, Marx means the states near the Mississippi River, such as Michigan, Illinois, and Iowa, not states further west. The war came about because the slaveholding oligarchy understood that Republican insistence on prohibiting slavery in the territories would doom slavery and exacerbate their conflicts with poor southern whites.

As the populations of the free states grow far more quickly than those of the slave states, the number of Northern Representatives was bound to outstrip that of the Southern very rapidly. The real seat of the political power of the South is . . . the American Senate, where every state . . . is represented by two Senators. In order to assert its influence in the Senate and, through the Senate, its hegemony over the United States, the South therefore required a continual formation of new slave states. This, however, was only possible through conquest of foreign lands . . . or through the transformation of the Territories belonging to the United States first into slave Territories and later into slave states . . . .

Finally, the number of actual slaveholders in the South of the Union does not amount to more than three hundred thousand, a narrow oligarchy that is confronted with many millions of so-called poor whites, whose numbers have been constantly growing through concentration of landed property . . . . Only by acquisition and the prospect of acquisition of new Territories . . . is it possible to square the interests of these poor whites with those of the slaveholders . . . , to tame them with the prospect of one day becoming slaveholders themselves. A strict confinement of slavery within its old terrain, therefore, was bound . . . to lead to its gradual effacement, in the political sphere to annihilate the hegemony that the slave states exercised through the Senate, and finally to expose the slaveholding oligarchy within its own states to threatening perils from the poor whites. In accordance with the principle that any further extension of slave Territories was to be prohibited by law, the Republicans therefore attacked the rule of the slaveholders at its root. The Republican election victory was accordingly bound to lead to open struggle between North and South . . . .

It did not escape the slaveholders that a new power had arisen, the Northwest, whose population, having almost doubled between 1850 and 1860, was already pretty well equal to the white population of the slave states—a power that was not inclined either by tradition, temperament or mode of life to let itself be dragged from compromise to compromise in the manner of the old North-eastern states. The Union was still of value to the South only so far as it handed over Federal power to it as a means of carrying out the slave policy. If not, then it was better to make the break now than to look on at the development of the Republican Party and the upsurge of the Northwest for another four years and begin the struggle under more unfavourable conditions . . . .

The whole movement was and is based, as one sees, on the slave question. Not in the sense of whether the slaves within the existing slave states should be emancipated outright or not, but whether the twenty million free men of the North should submit any longer to an oligarchy of three hundred thousand slaveholders; whether the vast Territories of the republic should be nurseries for free states or for slavery . . . .

Marx, "The Civil War in the United States."[11]

Two weeks later, on November 7, Marx continued his Die Presse *analysis of secession and slavery. He began by attacking the idea that the Union should allow the Confederacy to peaceably form a new nation. The war the Confederacy began was a true "war of conquest" that aimed to perpetuate and expand slavery. Far from a peaceable division, it wanted take over three-quarters of the United States, leaving the free states a small rump in the Northeast and its workers forced into a kind of slavery. Marx gleaned this exaggerated account from reports in American newspapers, particularly those of anti-slavery leanings.*

The advice of an amicable separation presupposes that the Southern Confederacy, although it assumed the offensive in the Civil War, at least wages it for defensive purposes[,] . . . that the issue for the slaveholders' party is merely one of uniting the territories it has hitherto dominated into an independent group of states . . . . Nothing could be more false. "*The South needs its entire territory. It will and must have it.*" With this battle-cry the secessionists fell upon Kentucky. By their "entire territory" they understand in the first place all the so-called *border states*—Delaware, Maryland, Virginia, North Carolina, Kentucky, Tennessee, Missouri and Arkansas.

Besides, they lay claim to the entire territory south of the line that runs from the northwest corner of Missouri to the Pacific Ocean. What the slaveholders, therefore, call the South, embraces more than three-quarters of the territory hitherto comprised by the Union . . . .

. . . [T]he war of the Southern Confederacy is in the true sense of the word a war of conquest for the spread and perpetuation of slavery. The greater part of the border states and Territories are still in the possession of the Union, whose side they have taken first through the ballot-box and then with arms. The Confederacy, however, counts them for the *"South"* and seeks to conquer them from the Union. In the border states which the Confederacy has occupied for the time being, it is holding the relatively free highlands in check by martial law. Within the actual slave states themselves it is supplanting the hitherto existing democracy by the unrestricted oligarchy of the 300,000 slaveholders . . . .

What would in fact take place would be not a dissolution of the Union, but a *reorganisation* of it . . . *on the basis of slavery* . . . . The plan of such a reorganisation has been openly proclaimed by the principal speakers of the South at the Congress of Montgomery . . . . The slave system would infect the whole Union. In the Northern states, where Negro slavery is in practice impossible, the white working class would gradually be forced down to the level of helotry [serfdom or slavery]. This would fully accord with the loudly proclaimed principle that only certain races are capable of freedom, and as the actual labour is the lot of the Negro in the South, so in the North it is the lot of the German and the Irishman, or their direct descendants.

With its expansionist goals, the Civil War was a struggle between slavery and free labor—and one that Northerners, even Democrats and anti-abolitionist conservatives recognized, deeming abolition an essential war goal, necessary to preserve the Union.

The present struggle between the South and North is, therefore, nothing but a struggle between two social systems, the system of slavery and the system of free labour. The struggle has broken out because the two systems can no longer live peacefully side by side on the North American continent. It can only be ended by the victory of one system or the other . . . .

. . . With the real war for the border states in the border states themselves, the question of winning or losing them is withdrawn from the sphere of diplomatic negotiations and parliamentary discussions. One section of slaveholders will throw off the mask of loyalty; the other will content itself with the prospect of a financial compensation such as Great Britain gave the West Indian planters. Events themselves drive to the promulgation of the decisive slogan—*emancipation of the slaves.*

That even the most hardened Democrats and diplomats of the North feel themselves drawn to this point, is shown by some announcements of very recent date . . . . In his last *Review* for October, Dr. [Orestes] *Brownson,* the spokesman of the Catholic party of the North, on his own admission the most energetic adversary of the emancipation movement from 1836 to 1860, publishes an article *for* Abolition. "If we have opposed Abolition heretofore," he says among other things, "because we would preserve the Union, we must *a fortiori* now oppose slavery whenever, in our judgement, its continuance becomes incompatible with the maintenance of the Union, or of our nation as a free republican state." Finally, the *World* . . . concludes one of its latest blustering articles against the Abolitionists with the words: "On the day when it shall be decided that either slavery or the Union must go down, on that day sentence of death is passed on slavery. If the North cannot triumph *without* emancipation, it will triumph *with* emancipation."

CHAPTER 4

Slavery, Emancipation, and the Progress of the Civil War, 1861-1862

MARX ON CONTRABANDS AND FREEDOM

As early as December 1861, Marx knew that the slavery was on its way to extinction, even if the ever-cautious Lincoln acted slowly. Some military commanders welcomed slaves into their camps or even declared all slaves freed; others chased them away. Lincoln watched as this happened, pulling commanders back when they overstepped. Lincoln could replace such caution with action, Marx related in a March 3, 1862, Die Presse piece about General McClelland's removal: "President Lincoln never ventures a step forward before the tide of circumstances and the general call of public opinion forbid further delay. But once 'Old Abe' realises that such a turning point has been reached, he surprises friend and foe alike by a sudden operation executed as noiselessly as possible."

Almost as soon as the Civil War began, slaves started to run to Union lines; large numbers gained freedom at the village of Hampton, Virginia. But the military situation made continued occupation there precarious, and military commanders ordered the troops and contrabands moved. "Contrabands" were the runaway slaves, given that name because by freeing themselves they became war contraband, which Union armies could seize and use. The illustration, from Harper's Weekly, August 17, 1861, relates what happened when the precariously freed slaves heard about the move to Fortress Monroe. Fearing that they would be left behind and desperate to maintain their precarious freedom, they began what the magazine called a "Stampede of Slaves to Fortress Monroe."

Elsewhere in the issue, the magazine reprinted an article from a New York Herald correspondent about the incident, excerpted on the following page. Note the racially tinged language ("laughable," "pitiful," "little picaninnies," "unfortunate creatures"), which painted the runaway slaves as inferior objects of pity and laughter—a reaction much like Lincoln's when confronted with the slave coffle.

Stampede of Slaves from Hampton to Fortress Monroe

"The Stampede from Hampton."[1]

The fear of an immediate attack from the rebels, and the bringing into servitude again of all the negroes, lent wings to the contrabands . . . , and the hasty preparations for instant flight, and the exodus that followed, were the most laughable and at the same time pitiable sight I ever witnessed. All awakened from their sleep, they seized such articles as they valued the most, and set out in the midnight hours, over a long and lonely road leading to the fort, for that haven in which they looked for comfort and safety that would not be again disturbed. First came the men, some of them bearing in their arms the little picaninnies, who cried and sobbed from fear; others toting household furniture upon their heads, hurrying along lest their masters should finally snatch them from their newly-found freedom, and again send them to the fields under the overseer's whip. Then came women, also bearing their clothes, furniture, bedding, and, in short, every thing that made up their household effects. Children of all ages, sizes, color, and appearance clung to the skirts of the venerable old negro women, who rushed hastily along the road, dragging the children after them, and sharply rebuking their cries and expressions of fear . . . .

The day broke, and still the road was traversed by contrabands, each one bearing a load on his or her head or wheeling a creaking barrow, or perhaps draining a cart loaded down with furniture.... At about ten o'clock I rode over to Hampton, to witness what was expected to be the destruction by fire of the entire village and bridge leading to it. At that time I met... hundreds of slaves, men, women, and children, the women invariably turbaned with a flaming bandana handkerchief, and the children barefooted and without covering to the head. Not a single article of furniture found in this latitude but might have been seen on the heads of these unfortunate creatures, and what was too heavy to carry was placed in the canoes, flatboats, and wherries that dotted the bay, pulled by swarthy sons of Africa. Never was such an exodus seen before in this country....

Marx, "The Crisis Over the Slavery Issue," Die Presse, December 14, 1861.[2]

The United States has evidently entered a critical stage with regard to the slavery question, the question underlying the whole Civil War. General Fremont has been dismissed for declaring the slaves of rebels free. A directive to General Sherman, the commander of the expedition to South Carolina... goes further than Fremont, for it decrees that fugitive slaves even of loyal slave-owners should be welcomed and employed as workers and paid a wage, and under certain circumstances armed, and consoles the "loyal" owners with the prospect of receiving compensation later. Colonel Cochrane... demands the arming of all slaves as a military measure... General Halleck, Fremont's successor in Missouri, and General Dix in east Virginia have driven fugitive Negroes from their military camps.... General Wool at the same time has received the black "contraband" with open arms at Fort Monroe.... The slavery question is being solved in practice in the border slave states even now, especially in Missouri and to a lesser extent in Kentucky, etc. A large-scale dispersal of slaves is taking place. For instance 50,000 slaves have disappeared from Missouri, some of them have run away, others have been transported by the slave-owners to the more distant southern states....

LINCOLN AND MARX ON EMANCIPATION AND THE CIVIL WAR

Lincoln, 1862 Message to Congress.[3]

Lincoln understood that the circumstance that Marx described—fervent disagreement among generals and cabinet officers about the fate of slaves, both in the Confederacy and in the loyal Border States—required resolution. In an address to Congress in early March 1862, he espoused a kind of gradual compensated emancipation policy that resembled what northern states had embraced in the late eighteenth century, plans that would keep freed slaves in a form of bondage for several decades.

Fellow-citizens of the Senate, and House of Representatives, I recommend the adoption of a Joint Resolution by your honorable bodies which shall be substantially as follows: "Resolved that the United States ought to co-operate with any state which may adopt gradual abolishment of slavery, giving to such state pecuniary aid, to be used by such state in its discretion, to compensate for the inconveniences public and private, produced by such change of system."

If the proposition contained in the resolution . . . does command . . . approval, I deem it of importance that the states and people immediately interested, should be at once distinctly notified of the fact, so that they may begin to consider whether to accept or reject it. The federal government would find its highest interest in such a measure, as one of the most efficient means of self-preservation. The leaders of the existing insurrection entertain the hope that this government will ultimately be forced to acknowledge the independence of some part of the disaffected region, and that all the slave states North of such part will then say "the Union, for which we have struggled, being already gone, we now choose to go with the Southern section." To deprive them of this hope, substantially ends the rebellion; and the initiation of emancipation completely deprives them of it, as to all the states initiating it. The point is not that all the states tolerating slavery would very soon, if at all, initiate emancipation; but that, while the offer is equally made to all, the more Northern shall, by such initiation, make it certain to the more Southern, that in no event, will the former ever join the latter, in their proposed confederacy. I say "initiation" because, in my judgment, gradual, and not sudden emancipation, is better for all. In the mere financial, or pecuniary view, any member of Congress, with the census-tables and Treasury-reports before him, can readily see for himself how very soon the current expenditures of this war would purchase, at fair valuation, all the slaves in any named State. Such a proposition, on the part of the general government, sets up no claim of a right, by federal authority, to interfere with slavery within state limits, referring, as it does, the absolute control of the subject, in each case, to the state and its people, immediately interested....

Marx, "A Treaty Against the Slave Trade," Die Presse, May 22, 1862.[4]

Marx interpreted an Anglo-American treaty on the Atlantic slave trade, one that freed all those enslaved on captured ships, along with the prohibition of the domestic slave trade, even in the Border States, as another sign that Lincoln had made abolition a key part of the war policy. Such a treaty, however, would not touch the mainsprings of the nineteenth-century Atlantic slave trade—the trade to Brazil and Cuba—unless ships bound for those places were captured.

The Treaty on the suppression of the slave trade concluded between the United States and Britain on April 7 . . . . Mixed courts, composed half of Englishmen, half of Americans . . . will pass judgment on the prize vessels. . . . Not only the presence of captive Negroes is regarded as affording legal grounds for the seizure of ships, but also special equipment in the ship for the traffic in Negroes, manacles, chains and other instruments for guarding the Negroes and, lastly, stores of provisions that greatly exceed the requirements of the ship's company . . . . The Negroes found on board convicted ships are . . . to be set at liberty at once and remain free under guarantee of the government in whose territory they find themselves . . . .

A mortal blow has been dealt the Negro trade by this Anglo-American Treaty—the result of the American Civil War. The effect of the Treaty will be completed by the Bill recently introduced by Senator Sumner . . . [that] punishes the transport of slaves from one port of the United States to another as a crime. This Bill does, to a large extent, paralyse the trade that the states raising Negroes (border slave states) are carrying on with the states consuming Negroes (the slave states proper).

LINCOLN ANNOUNCES THE EMANCIPATION PROCLAMATION

Lincoln, First Draft, Emancipation Proclamation.[5]

President Lincoln first presented a draft of the Emancipation Proclamation to the cabinet in July 1862, two months after Marx reported on the slave trade treaty. This draft, shorter than either the preliminary or final Emancipation Proclamation, emphasized military necessity and reiterated his offer to help any state that pursued gradual emancipation. The cabinet dissented, some wanting more vigorous action, others seeking to postpone it to a more favorable time.

In pursuance of the . . . act of congress entitled "An act to suppress insurrection and to punish treason and rebellion, to seize and confiscate property of rebels, and for other purposes" . . . , I, ABRAHAM LINCOLN, President of the United States, do hereby proclaim to, and warn all persons . . . to cease participating in, aiding, countenancing, or abetting the existing rebellion, or any rebellion against the government of the United States, and to return to their proper allegiance to the United States, on pain of the forfeitures and seizures, as within . . . provided.

And I hereby make known that it is my purpose, upon the next meeting of congress, to again recommend the adoption of a practical measure for tendering pecuniary aid to the free choice or rejection, of any and all States which may then be recognizing and practically sustaining the authority of the United States, and which may . . . voluntarily adopt, gradual abolishment of slavery . . . —that the object is to practically restore, thenceforward to be maintained, the constitutional relation between the general government, and each, and all the states, wherein that relation is now suspended, or disturbed; and that, for this object, the war, as it has been, will be, prosecuted. And, as a fit and necessary military measure for effecting this object, I, as Commander-in-Chief of the Army and Navy of the United States, do order and declare that on the first day of January in the year of Our Lord one thousand, eight hundred and sixty-three, all persons held as slaves within any state or states, wherein the constitutional authority of the United States shall not then be practically recognized, submitted to, and maintained, shall then, thenceforward, and forever, be free . . . .

1860 US Census Map.[6]

Francis Bicknell Carpenter placed a map in the lower right corner of his 1864 painting, "First Reading of the Emancipation Proclamation of President Lincoln." That map, entitled "the distribution of the slave population of the southern states of the United States compiled from the Census of 1860," appeared in September 1861 (see p. 71). Cartographer Edwin Hergesheimer, of the United States Coastal Survey, headed a team that made the map. Like others employed by the coastal survey, he had left Germany after the suppression of the 1848 democratic revolution. He and his émigré colleagues opposed slavery; they made the map during the secession crisis, as a tool to persuade states like Virginia and Tennessee to stay in the Union.

Lincoln used the map to aid emancipation policy and track military strategy. The map sustained his gradual emancipation policy, for it showed that that most sections of the Border States had a low percentage of slaves in the population, less than 20 percent, save for a few enclaves. It showed Confederate strongholds with dense slave populations. Invading such counties would inflict the greatest damage on the Confederacy by encouraging slaves to run away and destroying farms that provided provisions to the Confederate army. Light-colored areas, mountain areas with less than 20 percent of the population enslaved, might have Unionist sentiment.

The map's innovative system of shading illustrated the density of slavery in each county in the slaveholding states. The map's key had nine shadings, from less than 10 percent enslaved (white) to over 80 percent (black); in addition, the map put the percentage of slaves inside the borders of each county. The blackest-shaded counties—the sugar parishes along the Mississippi River, the "black belt" cotton counties, the rice coast of South Carolina and Georgia—had made the earliest commitment to the Confederacy. A table at the bottom of the map listed the free and slave populations, and percentage of the population enslaved in every slaveholding state.

The seemingly neutral map thus supported emancipation. It connected slavery to rebellion so directly that every user would see it. Its very title presumed that the Confederate states remained part of the Union; the proceeds from its sale went to the "sick and wounded soldiers of the Union Army." Even the statistical table took on an abolitionist hue: instead of separating free blacks from slaves, it included all free people, white and black, together, thus suggesting the equality of all free people.

MARX ON EMANCIPATION

Marx, "A Criticism of American Affairs," August 1862.[7]

In summer 1862, a month before Lincoln announced the Emancipation Proclamation (but after he presented a draft to his cabinet that Marx could not have known about),

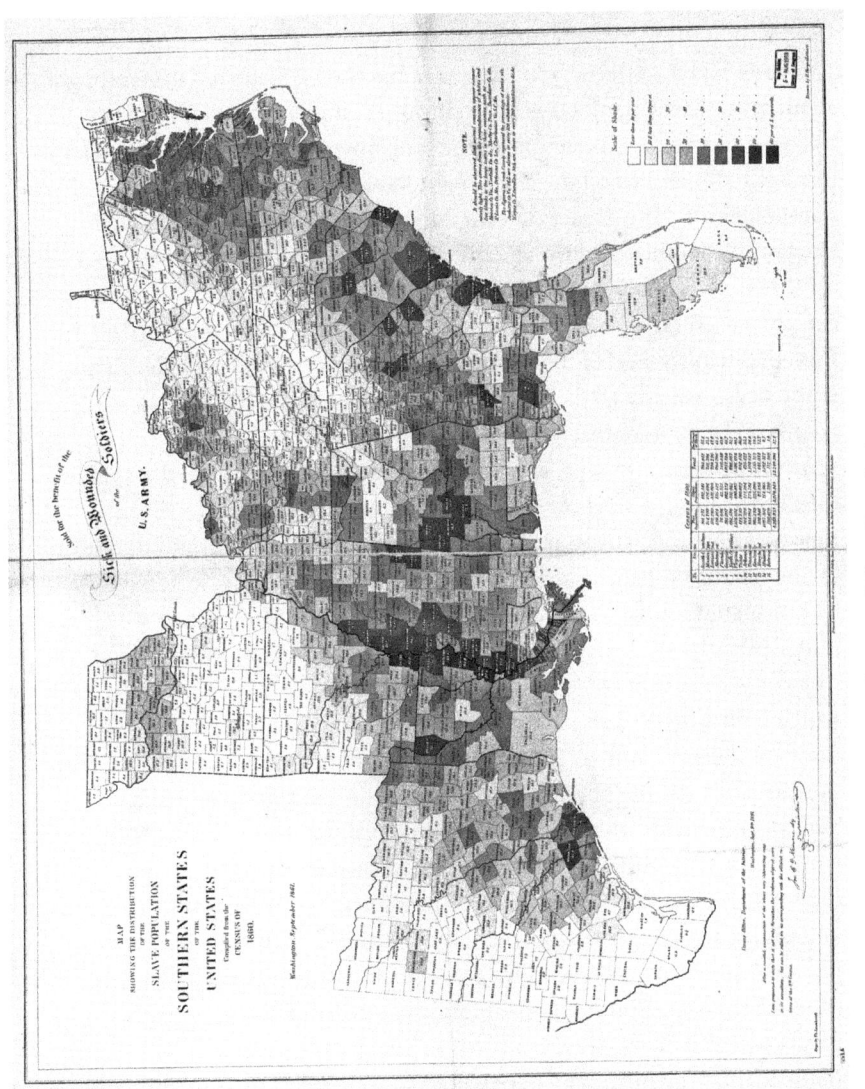

Distribution of Slave Population, 1860

Marx saw continued crisis in the Union, one brought on by Lincoln's desire to placate the Border States: slaves were prevented from serving in the Union army. Furthermore, New Englanders or those in the Northwest would not enlist until he made the war one about the abolition of slavery.

The crisis, which at the moment reigns in the United States has been brought about by two causes: military and political.... It is anxious regard for the wishes, advantages and interests of the spokesmen of the border slave states that has so far broken off the Civil War's point of principle.... The "loyal" slaveholders of these border states saw to it that the fugitive slave laws dictated by the South ... were maintained and the sympathies of the Negroes for the North forcibly suppressed, that no general could venture to put a company of Negroes in the field and that slavery was finally transformed from the Achilles' heel of the South into its invulnerable horny hide. Thanks to the slaves, who do all the productive work, all able-bodied men in the South can be put into the field!

At the present moment, when secession's stocks are rising, the spokesmen of the border states are making even greater claims. However, Lincoln's appeal to them, in which he threatens them with inundation by the Abolition party, shows that things are taking a revolutionary turn. Lincoln knows ... that it is by no means apathy or giving way under pressure of defeat that causes his demand for 300,000 recruits to meet with such a cold response. New England and the Northwest, which have provided the main body of the army, are determined to force on the government a revolutionary kind of warfare and to inscribe the battle-slogan of "Abolition of Slavery!" on the star-spangled banner. Lincoln yields only hesitantly and uneasily to this pressure from without, but he knows that he cannot resist it for long. Hence his urgent appeal to the border states to renounce ... slavery voluntarily and under advantageous contractual conditions. He knows that only the continuance of slavery in the border states has so far left slavery untouched in the South and prohibited the North from applying its great radical remedy. He errs only if he imagines that the "loyal" slaveholders are to be moved by benevolent speeches and rational arguments. They will yield only to force....

Meanwhile, during its first session Congress ... abolished slavery in ... the national capital, with monetary compensation for the former slaveholders. Slavery was declared "forever impossible" in all the Territories of the United States. The Act, under which the new State of West Virginia is admitted into the Union, prescribes abolition of slavery by stages and declares that all Negro children born after July 4, 1863, are born free . . . . By a fourth Act all the slaves of rebels are to be emancipated, as soon as they fall into the hands of the republican army. Another law, which is now being put into effect for the first time, provides that these emancipated Negroes may be militarily organised and put into the field against the South. The independence of the Negro republics of Liberia and Haiti has been recognised and, finally, a treaty on the abolition of the slave trade has been concluded with Britain. Thus, no matter how the dice may fall in the fortunes of war, even now it can safely be said that Negro slavery will not long outlive the Civil War.

Marx To Engels, August 7, 1862.[8]

Though Marx thought the Union would eventually emerge victorious, he did think the Union should cease fighting a "constitutional" war and begin a "revolutionary" one that enshrined abolition as its key goal.

. . . From the outset, the NORTHERNERS have been dominated by . . . the BORDER SLAVE STATES . . . . The South . . . acted as a single whole right from the very start. The North itself turned slavery into a pro- instead of an anti-Southern military FORCE. The South leaves PRODUCTIVE LABOUR to the slaves and could thus take the field undisturbed with its fighting force intact . . . . In my view, all this is going to TAKE ANOTHER TURN. The North will, at last, wage the war in earnest, have recourse to revolutionary methods and overthrow the supremacy of the border slave statesmen. One single N[EGRO] REGIMENT would have a remarkable effect on Southern nerves.

The difficulty of raising 300,000 men is . . . purely political. The North-West and New England wish to and will compel the government to abandon the diplomatic warfare they have waged hitherto, and are now making TERMS ON WHICH THE 300,000 MEN SHALL COME FORTH. If Lincoln doesn't give way (which he will, however), there'll be a revolution . . . . The long and the short of it is, I think, that wars of this kind ought to be conducted along revolutionary lines, and the Yankees have so far been trying to conduct it along constitutional ones.

LINCOLN: TOWARD EMANCIPATION AND COLONIZATION

Lincoln, "Address on Colonization."[9]

While Marx speculated on the future of abolition, Lincoln drafted his proclamation freeing slaves. On August 14, 1862, after discussing the preliminary Emancipation Proclamation with his cabinet, he invited free black men who lived in Washington, DC to listen to him demand they support colonization of freed people. His comments expose the race consciousness of white anti-slavery advocates: slavery hurt whites as much as those enslaved; the two races, shackled together by slavery must live separately; whites will never allow black people equality; all but a tiny number of those of African descent were inferior to whites; ex-slaves had no extended families or communities where they might thrive in freedom in the United States.

... The President ... informed them that a sum of money had been appropriated by Congress ... for ... aiding the colonization in some country of the people, or a portion of them, of African descent, thereby making it his duty, as it had for a long time been his inclination, to favor that cause; and why, he asked, should the people of your race be colonized, and where? Why should they leave this country...? You and we are different races. We have between us a broader difference than exists between almost any other two races. Whether it is right or wrong I need not discuss, but this physical difference is a great disadvantage to us both, as I think your race suffer very greatly, many of them by living among us, while ours suffer from your presence....

Perhaps you have long been free, or all your lives. Your race are suffering, in my judgment, the greatest wrong inflicted on any people. But even when you cease to be slaves, you are yet far removed from being placed on an equality with the white race. You are cut off from many of the advantages which the other race enjoy. The aspiration of men is to enjoy equality with the best when free, but on this broad continent, not a single man of your race is made the equal of a single man of ours. Go where you are treated the best....

I do not propose to discuss this, but to present it as a fact with which we have to deal. I cannot alter it if I would. It is a fact, about which we all think and feel alike, I and you. We look to our condition, owing to the existence of the two races on this continent. I need not recount to you the effects upon white men, growing out of the institution of Slavery. I believe in its general evil effects on the white race. See our present condition—the country engaged in war!—our white men cutting one another's throats.... But for your race among us there could not be war.... [W]ithout the institution of Slavery and the colored race as a basis, the war could not have an existence.

It is better for us both, therefore, to be separated. I know that there are free men among you, who even if they could better their condition are not as much inclined to go out of the country as those, who being slaves could obtain their freedom on this condition. I suppose one of the principal difficulties in the way of colonization is that the free colored man cannot see that his comfort would be advanced by it. You may believe you can live in Washington or elsewhere in the United States the remainder of your life as easily... than you can in any foreign country, and hence you may come to the conclusion that you have nothing to do with the idea of going to a foreign country. This is... an extremely selfish view of the case.

But you ought to... help those who are not so fortunate as yourselves. There is an unwillingness on the part of our people, harsh as it may be, for you free colored people to remain with us. Now, if you could give a start to white people, you would open a wide door for many to be made free. If we deal with those who are not free at the beginning, and whose intellects are clouded by Slavery, we have very poor materials to start with. If intelligent colored men, such as are before me, would move in this matter, much might be accomplished. It is exceedingly important that we have men at the beginning capable of thinking as white men, and not those who have been systematically oppressed.... For the sake of your race you should sacrifice... your present comfort....

Lincoln suggested both Liberia (with its tiny population of American-born people of color and their descendants) and Central American countries (none of which would accept the immigrants). Knowing few would leave the country, he pressed his listeners to persuade as few as twenty-five people to emigrate.

... Liberia has been in existence a long time. In a certain sense it is a success. The old President of Liberia, Roberts, has just been with me.... He says they have within the bounds of that colony between 300,000 and 400,000 people.... Something less than 12,000 have been sent thither from this country. Many of the original settlers have died, yet, like people elsewhere, their offspring outnumber those deceased. The question is if the colored people are persuaded to go anywhere, why not there? One reason for an unwillingness to do so is that some of you would rather remain within reach of the country of your nativity. I do not know how much attachment you may have toward our race. It does not strike me that you have the greatest reason to love them....

The place I am thinking about having for a colony is in Central America. It is nearer to us than Liberia ... within seven days' run by steamers.... The country is a very excellent one for any people, and with great natural resources and advantages, and especially because of the similarity of climate with your native land—thus being suited to your physical condition.... [T]his particular place has all the advantages for a colony. On both sides there are harbors among the finest in the world. Again, there is evidence of very rich coal mines.... [C]oal ... will afford an opportunity to the inhabitants for immediate employment till they get ready to settle permanently in their homes....

... I want to ascertain [if] ... I can get a number of able-bodied men, with their wives and children, who are willing to go, when I present evidence of encouragement and protection. Could I get a hundred tolerably intelligent men, with their wives and children, to "cut their own fodder," so to speak? Can I have fifty? If I could find twenty-five able-bodied men, with a mixture of women and children, good things in the family relation, I think I could make a successful commencement.... [L]et me know whether this can be done or not. This is the practical part of my wish to see you....

Frederick Douglass, "The President and His Speeches."[10]

Lincoln's free black auditors, and their followers, angrily rejected his offer. Frederick Douglass, the most famous runaway slave in America, excoriated Lincoln's address. Douglass's powerful language, written soon after the event, suggests that Lincoln could not please free blacks and white, northern voters at the same time.

Mr. Lincoln assumes the language and arguments of an itinerant Colonization lecturer, showing all his inconsistencies, his pride of race and blood, his contempt for negroes and his canting hypocrisy.... The argument of Mr. Lincoln is that the difference between the white and black races renders it impossible for them to live together in the same country without detriment to both. Colonization therefore, he holds to be the duty and the interest of the colored people....

A horse thief pleading that the existence of the horse is the apology for his theft or a highway man contending that the money in the traveler's pocket is the sole first cause of his robbery are about as much entitled to respect as is the President's reasoning.... No, Mr. President, it is not the innocent horse that makes the horse thief, not the traveler's purse that makes the highway robber, and it is not the presence of the negro that causes this foul and unnatural war, but the cruel and brutal cupidity of those who wish to possess horses, money and negroes by means of theft, robbery, and rebellion. Mr. Lincoln further knows or ought to know at least that negro hatred and prejudice of color are neither original nor invincible vices, but merely the offshoots of that root of all crimes and evils—slavery. If the colored people instead of having been stolen and forcibly brought to the United States had come as free immigrants, like the German and the Irish, never thought of as suitable objects of property, they never would have become the objects of aversion and bitter persecution, nor would there ever have been divulged and propagated the arrogant and malignant nonsense about natural repellancy and the incompatibility of races.

Lincoln to Greeley, August 22, 1862.[11]

Horace Greeley, who neither knew of Lincoln's plans nor understood the structural imperatives Marx thought would inevitably end slavery, lambasted Lincoln for failing to emancipate the slaves. In a missive published in the New-York Tribune *on August 19, 1862, entitled "The Prayer of the Twenty Millions," he argued that Lincoln had listened too often to Border State politicians and had rebuked those generals who sought to free slaves who ran away to their lines. In an extraordinarily disingenuous response, Lincoln pretended his position on slavery and freedom had not changed since his election; he did not reveal he had the Emancipation Proclamation in his pocket, waiting for the right time to release it.*

As to the policy I "seem to be pursuing" as you say, I have not meant to leave any one in doubt. I would save the Union. I would save it the shortest way under the Constitution. The sooner the national authority can be restored; the nearer the Union will be "the Union as it was." If there be those who would not save the Union, unless they could at the same time save slavery, I do not agree with them. If there be those who would not save the Union unless they could at the same time destroy slavery, I do not agree with them. My paramount object in this struggle is to save the Union, and is not either to save or to destroy slavery. If I could save the Union without freeing any slave I would do it, and if I could save it by freeing all slaves I would do it; and if I could save it by freeing some and leaving others alone I would also do that. What I do about slavery, and the colored race, I do because I believe it helps to save the Union; and what I forbear, I forbear because I don't believe it would help to save the Union. I shall do less whenever I shall believe what I am doing hurts the cause, and I shall do more whenever I shall believe doing more will help the cause. I shall try to correct errors when shown to be error; and I shall adopt new views so fast as they shall appear to be true views. I have here stated my purpose according to my view of Official duty: and I intend no modification of my oft-expressed personal wish that all men everywhere could be free.

Lincoln, "Reply to Emancipation Memorial Presented by Chicago Christians."[12]

Moderate Republicans hailed Lincoln's statement; abolitionist Wendell Phillips called it "[t]he most disgraceful document that ever came from the head of a free people." On September 13, 1862, when Lincoln saw a delegation of Chicago clergy who supported slave emancipation, he continued to hide his intentions, arguing that men of faith and anti-slavery congressmen disagreed about emancipation and—given military setbacks—the time was not ripe for such a declaration. The "Pope's bull against the comet" refers to the apocryphal story that Pope Callixtus III supposedly excommunicated Haley's Comet on its 1456 appearance, to assure a victory over the Ottoman Empire's armies. Perhaps to undercut the abolitionist reaction to his response to Greeley, he nonetheless made clear his anti-slavery sentiments. A report of Lincoln's response to the Chicago clergy reached print, in the September 23 Chicago Tribune, one day after he issued the Preliminary Emancipation Proclamation.

The subject presented in the memorial is one upon which I have thought much.... I am approached with the most opposite opinions and advice, and that by religious men, who are equally certain that they represent the Divine will. I am sure that either the one or the other class is mistaken in that belief.... I must study the plain physical facts of the case, ascertain what is possible and learn what appears to be wise and right. The subject is difficult, and good men do not agree. For instance, the other day four gentlemen of standing and intelligence ... from New York called, as a delegation, on business connected with the war; but, before leaving, two of them earnestly beset me to proclaim general emancipation, upon which the other two at once attacked them! You know, also, that the last session of Congress had a decided majority of anti-slavery men, yet they could not unite on this policy. And the same is true of the religious people . . . .

What good would a proclamation of emancipation from me do, especially as we are now situated? I do not want to issue a document that the whole world will see must necessarily be inoperative, like the Pope's bull against the comet! Would my word free the slaves, when I cannot even enforce the Constitution in the rebel States? Is there a single court, or magistrate, or individual that would be influenced by it there? And what reason is there to think it would have any greater effect upon the slaves than the late law of Congress . . . , which offers protection and freedom to the slaves of rebel masters who come within our lines? Yet I cannot learn that that law has caused a single slave to come over to us. And suppose they could be induced by a proclamation of freedom from me to throw themselves upon us, what should we do with them? How can we feed and care for such a multitude? Gen. Butler wrote me a few days since that he was issuing more rations to the slaves who have rushed to him than to all the white troops under his command . . . . If, now, the pressure of the war should call off our forces from New Orleans to defend some other point, what is to prevent the masters from reducing the blacks to slavery again; for . . . whenever the rebels take any black prisoners, free or slave, they immediately auction them off! . . . For instance, when, after the late battles at and near Bull Run, an expedition went out from Washington under a flag of truce to bury the dead and bring in the wounded, and the rebels seized the blacks who went along to help and sent them into slavery, Horace Greeley said in his paper that the Government would probably do nothing about it. What could I do? . . .

Now, then, tell me, if you please, what possible result of good would follow the issuing of such a proclamation as you desire? Understand, I raise no objections against it on legal or constitutional grounds; for, as commander-in-chief of the army and navy, in time of war, I suppose I have a right to take any measure which may best subdue the enemy. Nor do I urge objections of a moral nature, in view of possible consequences of insurrection and massacre at the South. I view the matter as a practical war measure, to be decided upon according to the advantages or disadvantages it may offer to the suppression of the rebellion . . . .

The clergy responded that proclaiming emancipation would make enforcing the Constitution in the South possible and would come into operation as Union armies succeeded. With new events on the ground, perhaps Congress would come to an agreement to support emancipation. It would, moreover, "secure the sympathy of Europe and the whole civilized world" while sending "a thrill through the entire North, giving the people a glorious principle for which to suffer and fight." In his answer, Lincoln admitted that slavery caused the war but dissented on arming blacks, fearing that their arms would soon be in rebel hands.

I admit that slavery is the root of the rebellion . . . . The ambition of politicians may have instigated them to act, but they would have been impotent without slavery as their instrument. I will also concede that emancipation would help us in Europe, and convince them that we are incited by something more than ambition. I grant further that it would help somewhat at the North . . . And then unquestionably it would weaken the rebels by drawing off their laborers, which is of great importance. But I am not so sure we could do much with the blacks. If we were to arm them, I fear that in a few weeks the arms would be in the hands of the rebels; and indeed thus far we have not had arms enough to equip our white troops . . . . Every day increases their Union feeling [whites in the Border States]. They are also getting their pride enlisted, and want to beat the rebels. Let me say one thing more: I think you should admit that we already have an important principle to rally and unite the people in the fact that constitutional government is at stake . . . .

Do not misunderstand me, because I have mentioned these objections. They indicate the difficulties that have thus far prevented my action in some such way as you desire. I have not decided against a proclamation of liberty to the slaves, but hold the matter under advisement. And I can assure you that the subject is on my mind, by day and night, more than any other. Whatever shall appear to be God's will I will do. I trust that, in the freedom with which I have canvassed your views, I have not in any respect injured your feelings.

CHAPTER 5

Emancipation and Its Discontents

LINCOLN'S EMANCIPATION PROCLAMATION

Carpenter, Six Months at the White House.[1]

In September 1862, after the Union military victory at Antietam, Abraham Lincoln issued his "Preliminary Emancipation Proclamation." Lincoln's official writings contain few insights into his internal struggles over emancipation and how he came to think it necessary to win the war. Artist Francis Carpenter who spent six months in 1864 in the White House, painting his First Reading of the Emancipation Proclamation, *published a memoir in 1866, reporting his conversations with Lincoln. The book read like the hagiography of a martyred president. But internal evidence suggests he did speak with Lincoln. His reports about Lincoln's decision about issuing the Emancipation Proclamation are probably trustworthy, if not completely accurate transcripts. The selection begins when Carpenter first talks to Lincoln about the origins of the Emancipation Proclamation. Double quotes are Lincoln's words; single quotes within double ones represent Lincoln's report to Carpenter of conversations he held.*

[H]e proceeded to give me a detailed account of the history and issue of the great proclamation. "It had got to be . . . midsummer, 1862. Things had gone on from bad to worse, until I felt that we had reached the end of our rope on the plan of operations we had been pursuing; that we had about played our last card, and must change our tactics, or lose the game! I now determined upon the adoption of the emancipation policy; and without consultation with, or the knowledge of the Cabinet, I prepared the original draft of the proclamation, and, after much anxious thought, called a Cabinet meeting upon the subject. This was the last of July, or the first part of the month of August, 1862." . . .

"This Cabinet meeting took place, I think, upon a Saturday . . . . I said to the Cabinet that I had resolved upon this step, and had not called them together to ask their advice, but to lay the subject-matter of a proclamation before them; suggestions as to which would be in order, after they had heard it read.... Secretary Chase wished the language stronger in reference to the arming of the blacks. Mr. Blair, after he came in, deprecated the policy, on the ground that it would cost the Administration the fall elections. Nothing, however, was offered that I had not already fully anticipated and settled..., until Secretary Seward spoke. He said in substance: 'Mr. President, I approve of the proclamation, but I question the expediency of its issue at this juncture. The depression of the public mind, consequent upon our repeated reverses, is so great that I fear... [i]t may be viewed as the last measure of an exhausted government, a cry for help....' His idea, said the President, was that it would be 'considered our last shriek on the retreat.'... 'Now,' continued Mr. Seward, 'while I approve the measure, I suggest, sir, that you postpone its issue, until you can give it to the country supported by military success, instead of issuing it, as would be the case now, upon the greatest disasters of the war!'... The wisdom of the view of the Secretary of State struck me with very great force. It was an aspect of the case that, in all my thought upon the subject, I had entirely overlooked. The result was that I put the draft of the proclamation aside... waiting for a victory. From time to time I added or changed a line, touching it up here and there, anxiously watching the progress of events.... Finally, came the week of the battle of Antietam. I determined to wait no longer. The news came, I think, on Wednesday, that the advantage was on our side. I... called the Cabinet together to hear it, and it was published the following Monday...."

Lincoln, Preliminary Emancipation Proclamation.[2]

Note the military justification for Lincoln's action: the president could emancipate the slaves of enemies in wartime. He again urged slave states in the Union to pass gradual abolition laws and supported colonization of those freed. Though the Proclamation, to take effect one hundred days later, would not free a single slave in areas still rebellious, it encouraged self-emancipation and insisted that military commanders do nothing to return runaway slaves to their masters. Following the Second Confiscation Act, he ordered all slaves of rebellious masters that fell into military hands to gain immediate freedom. At a later time, he would send to Congress an act to compensate masters loyal to the Union for slaves thus freed.

A Proclamation. I, Abraham Lincoln, President of the United States of America, and Commander-in-Chief of the Army and Navy thereof, do hereby proclaim and declare that ... the war will be prosecuted for the object of practically restoring the constitutional relation between the United States, and each of the States, and the people thereof, in which States that relation is, or may be, suspended or disturbed.

That it is my purpose, upon the next meeting of Congress to again recommend the adoption of a practical measure tendering pecuniary aid to the free acceptance or rejection of all slave States, so called, the people whereof may not then be in rebellion against the United States and which States may then have voluntarily adopted, or thereafter may voluntarily adopt, immediate or gradual abolishment of slavery within their respective limits; and that the effort to colonize persons of African descent, with their consent, upon this continent, or elsewhere, with the previously obtained consent of the Governments existing there, will be continued.

That on the first day of January in the year of our Lord, one thousand eight hundred and sixty-three, all persons held as slaves within any State, or designated part of a State, the people whereof shall then be in rebellion against the United States shall be then, thenceforward, and forever free; and the executive government of the United States, including the military and naval authority thereof, will recognize and maintain the freedom of such persons, and will do no act or acts to repress such persons, or any of them, in any efforts they may make for their actual freedom.

That the executive will, on the first day of January aforesaid, by proclamation, designate the States, and part of States, if any, in which the people thereof respectively, shall then be in rebellion against the United States; and the fact that any State, or the people thereof shall, on that day be, in good faith represented in the Congress of the United States, by members chosen thereto, at elections wherein a majority of the qualified voters of such State shall have participated, shall, in the absence of strong countervailing testimony, be deemed conclusive evidence that such State and the people thereof, are not then in rebellion against the United States . . .

Lincoln then quoted from two congressional acts, one that added an article of war, approved March 13, 1862, and the other a July 17, 1862, act meant to suppress the rebellion.

"All officers or persons in the military or naval service of the United States are prohibited from employing any of the forces under their respective commands for the purpose of returning fugitives from service or labor, who may have escaped from any persons to whom such service or labor is claimed to be due, and any officer who shall be found guilty by a court martial of violating this article shall be dismissed from the service . . . ."

Also to . . . an act entitled "An Act to suppress Insurrection, to punish Treason and Rebellion, to seize and confiscate property of rebels, and for other purposes," approved July 17, 1862 . . . . "Sec.9. And be it further enacted, That all slaves of persons who shall hereafter be engaged in rebellion against the government of the United States, or who shall in any way give aid or comfort thereto, escaping from such persons and taking refuge within the lines of the army; and all slaves captured from such persons or deserted by them and coming under the control of the government of the United States; and all slaves of such persons found on (or) being within any place occupied by rebel forces and afterwards occupied by the forces of the United States, shall be deemed captives of war, and shall be forever free of their servitude and not again held as slaves.

"Sec.10. And be it further enacted, That no slave escaping into any State, Territory, or the District of Columbia, from any other State, shall be delivered up, or in any way impeded or hindered of his liberty, except for crime, or some offence against the laws, unless the person claiming said fugitive shall first make oath that the person to whom the labor or service of such fugitive is alleged to be due is his lawful owner, and has not borne arms against the United States in the present rebellion, nor in any way given aid and comfort thereto; and no person engaged in the military or naval service of the United States shall, under any pretence whatever, assume to decide on the validity of the claim of any person to the service or labor of any other person, or surrender up any such person to the claimant, on pain of being dismissed from the service."

And I do hereby enjoin upon and order all persons engaged in the military and naval service of the United States to observe, obey, and enforce, within their respective spheres of service, the act, and sections above recited. And the executive will in due time recommend that all citizens of the United States who shall have remained loyal thereto throughout the rebellion, shall (upon the restoration of the constitutional relation between the United States, and their respective States, and people, if that relation shall have been suspended or disturbed) be compensated for all losses by acts of the United States, including the loss of slaves . . . .

Carpenter, Six Months at the White House.[3]

Lincoln told Francis Carpenter, days after Congress sent to the states the Thirteenth Amendment making slavery unconstitutional for ratification, that this action had been the most significant of his presidency and the most important of the nineteenth century.

In February 1865, a few days after the passage of the "Constitutional Amendment," I went to Washington, and was received by Mr. Lincoln with the kindness and familiarity which had characterized our previous intercourse. I said to him at this time that I was very proud to have been the artist to have first conceived of the design of painting a picture commemorative of the Act of Emancipation; that subsequent occurrences had only confirmed my own first judgment of that act as the most sublime moral event in our history. "Yes," said he,—and never do I remember to have noticed in him more earnestness of expression or manner,—"as affairs have turned, it is the central act of my administration, and the great event of the nineteenth century."

MARX'S REACTION TO LINCOLN'S EMANCIPATION PROCLAMATION

Marx, "Comments on North American Events," October 1862.[4]

Three weeks later, in an article for Die Presse, *Karl Marx examined both the Battle of Antietam and the Preliminary Emancipation Proclamation. London newspapers screamed that the Proclamation would lead to a race war and bloody massacres; the* London Times *insisted in October 1862 that "the reign of the last PRESIDENT" would "go out amid horrible massacres of white women and children, to be followed by the extermination of the black race in the South." The* Times *asked, "Is LINCOLN yet a name not known to us as it will be known to posterity, and is it ultimately to be classed among that catalogue of monsters, the wholesale assassins and butchers of their kind?"*[5]

Although Marx admitted that Lincoln's language in the Proclamation resembled that of a lawyer's brief, he nonetheless insisted on the world historical significance of the Proclamation. He argued that it tore up the Constitution to end slavery, a point that constitutionalist Lincoln would have rejected. Marx portrays Lincoln as a man of the people, who lacked intellect or an "outstanding character," who barely understood the forces swirling around him, a stone-breaker who became president. This willful mischaracterization of Lincoln meant to turn him into a proletarian. Yet Lincoln would rank, Marx accurately predicted, with George Washington as a great president.

The short campaign in Maryland has decided the fate of the American Civil War.... [T]he fight for the possession of the border slave states is a fight for the domination over the Union, and the Confederacy has been defeated in this fight....

Lincoln's proclamation is even more important than the Maryland campaign. Lincoln is *a sui generis* [unique] figure in the annals of history. He has no initiative, no idealistic impetus..., no historical trappings. He gives his most important actions always the most commonplace form. Other people claim to be "fighting for an idea," when it is for them a matter of square feet of land. Lincoln, even when he is motivated by, an idea, talks about "square feet."... The most redoubtable decrees—which will always remain remarkable historical documents—flung by him at the enemy all look like, and are intended to look like, routine summonses sent by a lawyer to the lawyer of the opposing party.... His latest proclamation, which is drafted in the same style, the manifesto abolishing slavery, is the most important document in American history since the establishment of the Union, tantamount to tearing up the old American Constitution.

Nothing is simpler than to show that Lincoln's principal political actions contain much that is aesthetically repulsive, logically inadequate, farcical in form and politically contradictory, as is done by, the English Pindars of slavery, *The Times, The Saturday Review* and tutti quanti [all the rest]. But Lincoln's place in the history of the United States and of mankind will, nevertheless, be next to that of Washington!...

Lincoln is not the product of a popular revolution. This plebeian, who worked his way up from stone-breaker to Senator in Illinois, without intellectual brilliance, without a particularly outstanding character, without exceptional importance—an average person of good will, was placed at the top by the interplay of the forces of universal suffrage unaware of the great issues at stake. The new world has never achieved a greater triumph than by this demonstration that, given its political and social organisation, ordinary people of good will can accomplish feats which only heroes could accomplish in the old world!

... Although Lincoln does not possess the grandiloquence of historical action, as an average man of the people he has its humour. When does he issue the proclamation declaring that from January 1, 1863, slavery in the Confederacy shall be abolished? At the very moment when the Confederacy as an independent state decided on "peace negotiations" at its Richmond Congress. At the very moment when the slave-owners of the border states believed that the invasion of Kentucky by the armies of the South had made "the peculiar institution" [slavery] just as safe as was their domination over their compatriot, President Abraham Lincoln in Washington.

Marx to Engels, October 29, 1862.[6]

Nearly a month later, Marx, writing to Engels, made similar points, and he added that Southerners loathed the Emancipation Proclamation and, even before Lincoln issued it, had moved out of Border States to protect their slave property. His points, based on his reading of newspapers (both Union and Confederate) and abolitionist sources, were exaggerated. Large planters did move their slaves when Union armies approached but not in "vast proportions"; little evidence exists for wide-scale breeding of slaves for sale, a perennial abolitionist argument.

. . . The fact that Lincoln promulgated the PROSPECTIVE emancipation decree at a time when the CONFEDERATES were advancing into Kentucky also shows that no further consideration is now being shown the loyal SLAVE HOLDERS in the BORDER STATES. The southward migration of SLAVE HOLDERS with their black chattel from Missouri, Kentucky, and Tennessee has already assumed vast proportions and if, as is certain, the struggle goes on a bit longer, the South will have lost all support there. The war itself has been instrumental in destroying its power in the border states, which, in the absence of any market for the BREEDING OF SLAVES or the INTERNAL SLAVE TRADE, have been daily loosening their ties with the South anyhow . . . .
The fury with which the Southerners are greeting Lincoln's acts is proof of the importance of these measures. Lincoln's acts all have the appearance of inflexible, clause-ridden conditions communicated by a lawyer to his opposite number. This does not, however, impair their historical import . . . .

Marx, Election Results, November 1862.[7]

The Republicans lost badly in the 1862 mid-term election, held down by poor battlefield results and by Lincoln's preliminary Emancipation Proclamation. Marx thought that if Lincoln had made common cause with abolitionists in 1860, as he did in 1862, he would have lost the earlier election. In 1862, strong Republican support in the Midwest and large minorities in New York presaged victory for the abolitionist cause, the southern sympathies of New York City and the rural northwestern hatred of slavery and slaves notwithstanding. By "abolitionist party," Marx meant "anti-slavery party," one whose policies of prohibiting slavery in the territories would ultimately lead to its end.

New York City, strongly corrupted by Irish rabble, actively engaged in the slave trade until recently, the seat of the American money market and full of holders of mortgages on Southern plantations, has always been decidedly "Democratic . . . ." The Irishman sees the Negro as a dangerous competitor. The efficient farmers in Indiana and Ohio hate the Negro almost as much as the slaveholder. He is a symbol, for them, of slavery and the humiliation of the working class, and the Democratic press threatens them daily with a flooding of their territories by "niggers" . . . [sic; used by Marx in English].

At the time Lincoln was elected (1860) there was no civil war, nor was the question of Negro emancipation on the order of the day. The Republican Party, then quite independent of the Abolitionist Party, aimed its 1860 electoral campaign solely at protesting against the extension of slavery into the Territories, but, at the same time, it proclaimed non-interference with the institution in the states where it already existed legally. If Lincoln had had *Emancipation of the Slaves* as his motto at that time, there can be no doubt that he would have been defeated . . . .

Matters were quite different in the latest election. The Republicans made common cause with the Abolitionists. They came out emphatically for immediate emancipation, whether for its own sake or as a means of ending the rebellion. If this circumstance is taken into account, the majority in favour of the government in Michigan, Illinois, Massachusetts, Iowa and Delaware, and the very significant minority vote it obtained in the states of New York, Ohio and Pennsylvania, are equally surprising. Before the war such a result would have been impossible, even in Massachusetts. All that is needed now is energy, on the part of the government and of the Congress that meets next month, for the Abolitionists, now identical with the Republicans, to have the upper hand everywhere, both morally and numerically . . . .

Marx to Lion Philips, November 29, 1864.[8]

In late 1864, Marx—looking back on the progress of emancipation—saw a gigantic revolution, one unprecedented in the modern world.

When you reflect ... how at the time of Lincoln's election 3½ years ago it was only a matter of making no further concessions to the slave-owners, whereas now the avowed aim, which has in part already been realised, is the abolition of slavery, one has to admit that never has such a gigantic revolution occurred with such rapidity. It will have a highly beneficial influence on the whole world.

THE ATTACK ON EMANCIPATION

Opponents of emancipation, both in Marx's London and Lincoln's America, disseminated their views in in widely circulated contemporary prints. John Tenniel, "Abe Lincoln's Last Card; Or, Rouge-et-Noir (Red and Black)" appeared in the conservative London humor magazine, Punch *in October 1862 (see p. 90). It suggested a desperate Lincoln issued the Emancipation Proclamation. The cartoon demonstrates the accuracy of Marx's analysis of British elite opinion on the war. It depicts Lincoln and Confederate President Jefferson Davis sitting at a table-top balanced on a barrel of gunpowder. The phrase "last card" referred to the Emancipation Proclamation. Playing that black card would, Tenniel argued, lead to the racial war and blood-bath the London press expected, early in 1863.*

Tenniel borrowed the phrase "last card" from an editorial in the London Times. *The* Times *had insisted neither Lincoln nor Lincoln and the Congress together had any right to free the slaves and thereby "destroy the South and all its social organization at a blow," nor did they have the military ability to do so. Rather, Lincoln acted as a crass politician: he had "separated himself from the moderate Republicans, and fully accepted the extreme policy of the violent zealots the party includes without combining with them. He has played his last card" by declaring "that in all the States that shall not have returned to the Union on the 1st of January the slaves shall after that date be free."*[9]

Fierce racial politics permeated both the 1862 and 1864 elections. The 1864 Democratic Party print (see p. 91) depicts a ball espousing "Universal Freedom," "One Constitution," and "One Destiny" that the Emancipation Proclamation had supposedly brought, headed by "Abraham Lincoln Pre." It shows interracial dancing, which would lead to interracial marriages, thus debasing society. The text reads, in part, "The Miscegenation Ball at the Headquarters of the Lincoln Central Campaign Club ... being a perfect facsimile of the room.... No sooner were the formal proceedings and speeches hurried through with, than the room was cleared for a 'negro ball,' which then and there took place! ... This fact We Certify, 'that on the floor during the progress of the ball were many of the

ABE LINCOLN'S LAST CARD; OR, ROUGE-ET-NOIR.

Abe Lincoln's Last Card

accredited leaders of the Black Republican party, thus testifying their faith by works in the hall and headquarters of their political gathering. There were Republican Office-Holders, and prominent men of various degrees, and at least one Presidential Elector On The Republican Ticket.'" Note that all the male dancers were white, all the female dancers black, and that both men and women were elegantly dressed. The elegant dress, along with the seeming racial equality on the dance floor, suggests a level of social amalgamation that most Republicans (including Lincoln) rejected. A different print even shows the more-tabooed mixing of a white woman and black man.[10]

Lincoln: "The Emancipation Proclamation," January 1, 1863.[11]

In his January 1, 1863, final Emancipation Proclamation, Abraham Lincoln first quoted from the preliminary Emancipation Proclamation and then listed the states and parts of states—not being under federal control—where slaves would be emancipated. He made significant changes as he revised his preliminary Proclamation. He authorized the army to enlist freedmen as soldiers, but, at the same time, he urged those freed to avoid violence, employers to pay "reasonable wages," and the army to recruit those freed by the Proclamation.

The Miscegenation Ball

... Now, therefore I, Abraham Lincoln, President of the United States, by virtue of the power in me vested as Commander-in-Chief, of the Army and Navy of the United States in time of actual armed rebellion against the authority and government of the United States, and as a fit and necessary war measure for suppressing said rebellion, do, on this first day of January, in the year of our Lord one thousand eight hundred and sixty-three, and in accordance with my purpose so to do publicly proclaimed for the full period of one hundred days, from the day first above mentioned [September 22, 1862], order and designate as the States and parts of States wherein the people thereof respectively, are this day in rebellion against the United States, the following, to wit ... :

[Lincoln listed all of Arkansas, Texas, Mississippi, Alabama, Florida, Georgia, South Carolina, and North Carolina along with parts of Louisiana and Virginia.]

And by virtue of the power, and for the purpose aforesaid, I do order and declare that all persons held as slaves within said designated States, and parts of States, are, and henceforward shall be free; and that the Executive government of the United States, including the military and naval authorities thereof, will recognize and maintain the freedom of said persons.

And I hereby enjoin upon the people so declared to be free to abstain from all violence, unless in necessary self-defence; and I recommend to them that, in all cases when allowed, they labor faithfully for reasonable wages. And I further declare and make known, that such persons of suitable condition, will be received into the armed service of the United States to garrison forts, positions, stations, and other places, and to man vessels of all sorts in said service. And upon this act, sincerely believed to be an act of justice, warranted by the Constitution, upon military necessity, I invoke the considerate judgment of mankind, and the gracious favor of Almighty God....

Lincoln to Major General McClelland, January 1863.[12]

Days after issuing the Emancipation Proclamation, Lincoln deemed it required by military necessity. His comments came in response to a letter from General McClelland, who had received peace feelers from friends in the Confederate military. He returned to the problem of slavery in the Border States and those regions the Union controlled. As early as November 1861, he had drafted a gradual abolition law for the Delaware legislature, but no state legislator introduced it. Neither he nor Congress could end slavery in these places, save with a constitutional amendment that outlawed the institution. He urged them to adopt a system of apprenticeship, a form of gradual abolition that might keep those born to enslaved mothers in bondage for decades after their birth (the Delaware draft law provided for an "apprenticeship" until eighteen for girls and twenty-one for boys). He included the states in rebellion, if they chose to return to the Union, a possibility Lincoln understood as highly unlikely.

After the commencement of hostilities I struggled nearly a year and a half to get along without touching the "institution" [slavery]; and when finally I conditionally determined to touch it, I gave a hundred days fair notice of my purpose, to all the States and people, within which time they could have turned it wholly aside, by simply again becoming good citizens of the United States. They chose to disregard it, and I made the peremptory proclamation on what appeared to me to be a military necessity. And being made, it must stand. As to the States not included in it, of course they can have their rights in the Union as of old. Even the people of the states included, if they choose, need not to be hurt by it. Let them adopt systems of apprenticeship for the colored people, conforming substantially to the most approved plans of gradual emancipation; and, with the aid they can have from the general government, they may be nearly as well off, in this respect, as if the present trouble had not occurred, and much better off than they can possibly be if the contest continues persistently.

As to any dread of my having a "purpose to enslave, or exterminate, the whites of the South," I can scarcely believe that such dread exists. It is too absurd. I believe you can be my personal witness that no man is less to be dreaded for undue severity, in any case. If the friends you mention really wish to have peace upon the old terms, they should act at once. Every day makes the case more difficult. They can so act, with entire safety, so far as I am concerned....

HARPER'S WEEKLY AND EMANCIPATION

Harper's Weekly *and Thomas Nast on Emancipation.*[13]

At first the Emancipation Proclamation left the vast majority of slaves in bondage— they either lived in the Border States or worked in areas the Union army had not liberated. But its symbolic significance to slaves who had learned about it had great immediate importance. The print at the top of page 95 appeared in Harper's Weekly *on January 24, 1863, three weeks after the Proclamation took effect. Columbia, who represented America, is at the top of the image. The center oval showed a freed family, dressed in well-made clothing, sitting in the parlor of their furnished home. Lincoln's portrait appears, indistinctly, above the mantle place. The right-hand side shows two vignettes of freedom: a mother sends her children off to a nearby school, and free workers are paid for their labor. Abolitionists long decried the way slavery made secure family life impossible and lamented that laws often prevented slaves from learning to read and write. Free labor, of course, stood at the center of Republican ideology. The left panels depict slavery as abolitionists and free blacks saw it: the top scene may show a slave sale, the bottom one a master or overseer whipping a slave.*

In 1865, probably after Lincoln's assassination, the image found below the first print reappeared as a print—with one great difference. The bottom-center cartouche replaced an abstract depiction of the divine origin of emancipation with a portrait of Abraham Lincoln, now—after most slaves had gained freedom—as the Great Emancipator. It probably represented the vision of white abolitionists—the people with the money to buy a print—as much as that of freed slaves. And it certainly ignored the slaves who had freed themselves by going to Union camps and the slaves freed by Union troops after the Proclamation went into effect.

LINCOLN ON THE FRUITS OF EMANCIPATION

Lincoln to Nathaniel P. Banks.[14]

The Emancipation Proclamation notwithstanding, President Lincoln feared that slaveholders in liberated areas might form state governments and attempt to preserve slavery in perpetuity. The Proclamation prohibited such action, and Lincoln, in a November 1863 letter to Union Major General Nathaniel P. Banks, in occupied Louisiana, informed him they had to abolish slavery to rejoin the Union.

Gov. Shepley has special instructions from the War Department. I wish him—these gentlemen and others co-operating—without waiting for more territory, to go to work and give me a tangible nucleus which the remainder of the State may rally around as fast as it can, and which I can at once recognize and sustain as the true State government. And in that work I wish you, and all under your command, to give them a hearty sympathy and support. The instruction to Gov. Shepley bases the movement . . . upon the loyal element. Time is important. There is danger, even now, that the adverse element seeks insidiously to pre-occupy the ground. If a few professedly loyal men shall draw the disloyal about them, and colorably set up a State government, repudiating the emancipation proclamation, and re-establishing slavery, I can not recognize or sustain their work . . . . This government, in such an attitude, would be a house divided against itself. I have said, and say again, that if a new State government, acting in harmony with this government, and consistently with general freedom, shall think best to adopt a reasonable temporary arrangement, in relation to the landless and homeless freed people, I do not object . . . .

Lincoln, "Annual Message to Congress, 1863."[15]

By late 1863, Lincoln reported progress in liberating rebel territory, freeing slaves, and enlisting freedmen. He insisted that none freed by the Proclamation or by the self-emancipation and military emancipation it encouraged would ever be re-enslaved, a point he emphatically repeated in a December 20, 1863, letter to abolitionist Henry C. Wright; he wrote, repeating word for word what Wright asked him to say: "I shall not attempt to retract or modify the emancipation proclamation; nor shall I return to

Thomas Nast, Emancipation, 1863

Thomas Nast, Emancipation, 1865

slavery any person who is free by the terms of that proclamation or by any of the acts of Congress."[16] *To sustain this policy, he insisted that the oath of loyalty given to rebels include acceptance of emancipation.*

... The policy of emancipation, and of employing black soldiers, gave to the future a new aspect, about which hope, and fear, and doubt contended in uncertain conflict. According to our political system . . . , the general government had no lawful power to effect emancipation in any State, and for a long time it had been hoped that the rebellion could be suppressed without resorting to it as a military measure. It was all the while deemed possible that the necessity for it might come, and that if it should, the crisis of the contest would then be presented. It came, and . . . it was followed by dark and doubtful days. Eleven months having now passed . . . . The rebel borders are pressed still further back, and by the complete opening of the Mississippi the country dominated by the rebellion is divided into distinct parts, with no practical communication between them. Tennessee and Arkansas have been substantially cleared of insurgent control, and influential citizens in each, owners of slaves and advocates of slavery at the beginning of the rebellion, now declare openly for emancipation in their respective States. Of those States not included in the emancipation proclamation, Maryland, and Missouri, neither of which three years ago would tolerate any restraint upon the extension of slavery into new territories, only dispute now as to the best mode of removing it within their own limits.

Of those who were slaves at the beginning of the rebellion, full one hundred thousand are now in the United States military service, about one-half of which number actually bear arms in the ranks; thus giving the double advantage of taking so much labor from the insurgent cause, and supplying the places which otherwise must be filled with so many white men. So far as tested, it is difficult to say they are not as good soldiers as any. No servile insurrection, or tendency to violence or cruelty, has marked the measures of emancipation and arming the blacks. These measures have been much discussed in foreign countries, and contemporary with such discussion the tone of public sentiment there is much improved . . . .

But if it be proper to require, as a test of admission to the political body, an oath of allegiance to the Constitution of the United States, and to the Union under it, why also to the laws and proclamations in regard to slavery? Those laws and proclamations were enacted and put forth for the purpose of aiding in the suppression of the rebellion. To give them their fullest effect, there had to be a pledge for their maintenance. In my judgment they have aided, and will further aid, the cause for which they were intended. To now abandon them would be not only to relinquish a lever of power, but would also be a cruel and an astounding breach of faith . . . . I shall not attempt to retract or modify the emancipation proclamation; nor shall I return to slavery any person who is free by the terms of that proclamation, or by any of the acts of Congress. For these and other reasons . . . support of these measures shall be included in the oath . . . .

Lincoln to Mary Mann, April 5, 1864 and Mann's response.[17]

Lincoln knew that the security of those freed by his edict remained precarious. Nor had he emancipated all slaves—slaves in areas under Union control on January 1, 1863, remained in bondage as did those in territories the Confederacy controlled. A better solution was needed—an amendment outlawing slavery entirely—as he intimated in an April 1864 letter to retired schoolteacher Mary Peabody Mann of Concord, Massachusetts, widow of education reformer Horace Mann. The short letter responded to a petition from Concord schoolchildren to free all children held as slaves.

The petition of persons under eighteen, praying that I would free all slave children, and the heading of which petition it appears you wrote, was handed me a few days since by Senator [Charles] Sumner [R-MA]. Please tell these little people I am very glad their young hearts are so full of just and generous sympathy, and that, while I have not the power to grant all they ask, I trust they will remember that God has, and that, as it seems, He wills to do it.

Mann responded to Lincoln that she would circulate his answer in the hopes that their prayers might be answered.

We intend immediately to scatter fac-similes of your sweet words to the children like apple blossoms all over the country—and we look with more hope than ever for the day when perfect justice shall be decreed, which shall make every able bodied colored man spring to the defence of the nation which it is plain the white man alone cannot save.

Lincoln, "Address at Sanitary Fair."[18]

A week after Lincoln answered Mary Mann, he spoke in Baltimore about the meaning of liberty for slaves. His parable of the sheep and the wolf made an unambiguous statement that all slaves deserved human liberty, a far stronger abolitionist argument than he had made before he saw freedmen's willingness to forge their own freedom through military service.

The world has never had a good definition of the word liberty, and the American people, just now, are much in want of one. We all declare for liberty; but in using the same word we do not all mean the same thing. With some the word liberty may mean for each man to do as he pleases with himself, and the product of his labor; while with others the same word may mean for some men to do as they please with other men, and the product of other men's labor. Here are two . . . incompatable things, called by the same name—liberty. And it follows that each of the things is, by the respective parties, called by two different and incompatable names—liberty and tyranny.

The shepherd drives the wolf from the sheep's throat, for which the sheep thanks the shepherd as a *liberator*, while the wolf denounces him for the same act as the destroyer of liberty, especially as the sheep was a black one. Plainly the sheep and the wolf are not agreed upon a definition of the word liberty; and precisely the same difference prevails to-day among us human creatures, even in the North, and all professing to love liberty. Hence we behold the processes by which thousands are daily passing from under the yoke of bondage, hailed by some as the advance of liberty, and bewailed by others as the destruction of all liberty . . . .

"Response to a Serenade."[19]

The New-York Tribune *reported on Lincoln's "Response to a Serenade," on February 3, 1865. Lincoln had hoped the Emancipation Proclamation would have led states to abolish slavery, but it had left much of the work of abolition incomplete. He expressed strong support to the crowd for the ratification of the Thirteenth Amendment, which abolished slavery. Congress had passed it; the amendment was then working its way through state legislatures.*

The President said he supposed the passage through Congress of the Constitutional amendment for the abolishment of Slavery throughout the United States, was the occasion to which he was indebted for the honor of this call.... The occasion was one of congratulation to the country and to the whole world. But there is a task yet before us—to go forward and consummate by the votes of the States that which Congress so nobly began yesterday.... He had the honor to inform those present that Illinois had already to-day done the work [i.e., ratified it]. Maryland was about half through; but he felt proud that Illinois was a little ahead. He thought this measure was a very fitting if not an indispensable adjunct to the winding up of the great difficulty. He wished the reunion of all the States perfected and so effected as to remove all causes of disturbance in the future; and to attain this end it was necessary that the original disturbing cause should, if possible, be rooted out. He thought all would bear him witness that he had never shrunk from doing all that he could to eradicate Slavery by issuing an emancipation proclamation.... But that proclamation falls far short of what the amendment will be when fully consummated. A question might be raised whether the proclamation was legally valid. It ... only aided those who came into our lines and that it was inoperative as to those who did not give themselves up, or that it would have no effect upon the children of the slaves born hereafter. In fact it would be urged that it did not meet the evil. But this amendment is a King's cure [a king's touch that cured disease] for all the evils. It winds the whole thing up. He would repeat that it was the fitting if not indispensable adjunct to the consummation of the great game we are playing. He could not but congratulate all present himself, the country and the whole world upon this great moral victory.

CHAPTER 6

Marx and Lincoln on the Fruits of the Civil War

MARX AND THE ENGLISH PROLETARIAT

Marx, "A London Workers' Meeting."[1]

English cotton factory owners and workers thought that the Union blockade of the Confederacy so reduced cotton imports into Great Britain that uncounted factory workers lost their jobs. (As noted below, the blockade was not the sole reason for declining cotton imports.) Nonetheless, as Marx knew, they had long supported the Union in the Civil War. As he reported in a dispatch to the Tribune, *the "working classes of England, from the commencement to the termination of the difficulty, have never forsaken them." Despite the economic consequences of the Union blockade on employment and unremitting pro-Confederacy rhetoric from the British press, during late 1861 and early 1862, British workers persisted in supporting the Union. An outpouring of British plebeian rallies favoring emancipation, at least fifty-six in number, took place during the first three months of 1863.*[2] *Marx explained the reasons for this support in a February 1862 dispatch in* Die Presse. *After asserting that the working class could influence public policy, despite its members not having parliamentary representation, he listed mass demonstrations that had led to Catholic emancipation, electoral reform, and a bill that mandated a ten-hour day, among others. He then turned to the Civil War.*

The misery that the stoppage of the factories and the shortening of the labour time, *motivated* by the blockade of the slave states, has produced among the workers in the northern manufacturing districts is incredible.... The other component parts of the working class do not suffer to the same extent; but they suffer severely from the reaction of the crisis in the cotton industry on the other industries, from the curtailment of the export of their own products to the North of America in consequence of the Morrill tariff and from the loss of this export to the South in consequence of the blockade . . . . English interference in America has accordingly become a knife-and-fork question for the working class. Moreover, no means of inflaming its wrath against the United States is scorned by its "natural superiors." . . . The working class is accordingly fully conscious that the government is only waiting for the intervention cry from below, the pressure from without, to put an end to the American blockade and English misery. Under these circumstances, the persistence with which the working class . . . breaks its silence only to raise its voice against intervention and for the United States, is admirable . . . .

Marx then reports a January 28, 1862, London meeting of the working class, held on the occasion of the eminent arrival of two Confederate agents. The meeting supported the Union as the only hope for the abolition of slavery. Those who spoke insisted that the agents meant to keep the slaves in chains. Support of the Confederacy would squander the money "this people"—the unemployed workers—had expended. As one speaker said:

"The two gentlemen . . . are the agents of slaveholding and tyrannical states. They are in open rebellion against the lawful Constitution of their country and come here to induce our government to recognise the independence of the slave states. It is the duty of the working class to pronounce its opinion now . . . . We must show that the money expended by this people on the emancipation of slaves cannot be allowed to be uselessly squandered. Had our government acted honestly, it would have supported the Northern states heart and soul in suppressing this fearful rebellion."

After a detailed defence of the Northern states . . . , the speaker proposed the following motion: "This meeting resolves that the agents of the rebels . . . now on the way from America to England, are absolutely unworthy of the moral sympathies of the working class of this country, since they are slaveholders as well as the confessed agents of the tyrannical faction that is at this very moment in rebellion against the American republic and the sworn enemy of the social and political rights of the working class in all countries . . . ."

After a representative of Confederate interests spoke, the motion received unanimous approval; when that representative protested, a second motion was raised and unanimously approved, along with another to send the meeting's proceedings to the American ambassador, Charles Francis Adams. The second motion, as reported by Marx, read:

"In view of the ill-concealed efforts of *The Times* and other misleading journals to misrepresent English public opinion on all American affairs; to embroil us in war with millions of our kinsmen on any pretext whatever, and to take advantage of the perils currently threatening the republic to defame democratic institutions, this meeting regards it as the very special duty of the workers . . . to declare their sympathy with the United States in their titanic struggle for the maintenance of the Union; to denounce the shameful dishonesty and advocacy of slaveholding on the part of *The Times* and kindred aristocratic journals . . . ; to express the warmest sympathy with the strivings of the Abolitionists for a final solution of the slave question."

Adams appreciated the support British workers gave to the Union cause. As he reported to Secretary of State William H. Seward in October 1862, he thought "that perhaps a majority of the poorer classes rather sympathize with us in our struggle, and it is only the aristocracy and the commercial body that are adverse." However much the British ministry wished to support the Confederacy, Adams concluded, this popular opinion prevented them from doing so.[3]

Marx, "Inaugural Address of the International Working Men's Association."[4]

At his October 1864 Inaugural Address to the International Working Men's Association, Marx linked slavery, the Civil War, and the immiseration of the proletariat. He compared the rapid growth of trade and rapid rise in the great fortunes of a few in Britain with the impoverishment of English and Irish workers, both in manufacturing and in agriculture, caused in part by the Union blockade of southern ports, which prevented import of cotton from the American South.

It is a great fact that the misery of the working masses has not diminished from 1848 to 1864, and yet this period is unrivaled for the development of its industry and the growth of its commerce. In 1850 a moderate organ of the British middle class . . . predicted that if the exports and imports of England were to rise 50 percent, English pauperism would sink to zero. Alas! On April 7, 1864, the Chancellor of the Exchequer delighted his parliamentary audience by the statement that the total import and export of England had grown in 1863 "to 443,955,000 pounds [59.6 billion 2014 US dollars]! That astonishing sum about three times the trade of the comparatively recent epoch of 1843! . . . When, consequent upon the Civil War in America, the operatives of Lancashire and Cheshire were thrown upon the streets, the same House of Lords sent to the manufacturing districts a physician commissioned to investigate into the smallest possible amount of carbon and nitrogen, to be administered in the cheapest and plainest form, which on an average might just suffice to "avert starvation diseases." Dr. Smith, the medical deputy, ascertained that 28,000 grains of carbon and 1,330 grains of nitrogen were the weekly allowance that would keep an average adult . . . just over the level of starvation diseases, and he found furthermore that quantity pretty nearly to agree with the scanty nourishment to which the pressure of extreme distress had actually reduced the cotton operatives . . . .

In nearly all of the rest of his speech (not reprinted here), he focused on the history and present class struggle between workers and capitalists and on the need of the working class to unite. Just before closing, he insisted that the working class had prevented Britain and other European powers from intervening in the Civil War and that the European working class aim for its own emancipation, thus linking the struggles of slaves for freedom and that of workers for a decent life. Marx concluded the speech with the following words.

Another conviction swayed that meeting. If the emancipation of the working classes requires their fraternal concurrence, how are they to fulfill that great mission with a foreign policy in pursuit of criminal designs, playing upon national prejudices, and squandering in piratical wars the people's blood and treasure? It was not the wisdom of the ruling classes, but the heroic resistance to their criminal folly by the working classes of England, that saved the west of Europe from plunging headlong into an infamous crusade for the perpetuation and propagation of slavery on the other side of the Atlantic.... The fight for such a foreign policy forms part of the general struggle for the emancipation of the working classes. Proletarians of all countries, unite!

MARX WRITES LINCOLN ON HIS REELECTION

Address of the International Working Men's Association to Abraham Lincoln, President of the United States of America Presented to U.S. Ambassador Charles Francis Adams. January 28, 1865.[5]

A month later, Marx composed a letter to Lincoln (written between November 22 and 29, 1864), for the International Workingmen's Association (which in 1872 became the first International of the Communist Party), congratulating him on his reelection to the presidency. Marx viewed Lincoln's reelection as a commitment to completing slave emancipation, and he thought emancipation and victory in the Civil War a precursor to the improvement of the proletariat worldwide. Not until all slaves had become free could workers, whatever their race, emancipate themselves from selling their labor power to capitalists.

The slaveholders' oligarchy stood, for Marx, in the same place as European aristocrats, tenuously clinging to power over the ascendant capitalist bourgeoisie. He deemed a victory of the capitalists over the aristocracy as a necessary first stage in the coming of a just communist social order. Marx paraphrased and quoted the Irish political economist and anti-slavery writer John Elliot Cairnes, The Slave Power: Its Character, Career, and Probable Designs ... (London: Parker, Bourn, and Son, 1862): 142-144, who had quoted and paraphrased Confederate Vice President Alexander Stephens's March 1861 Cornerstone speech. Note that Marx repeated his erroneous assertion that Lincoln was a "single-minded son of the working class."

Sir: We congratulate the American people upon your re-election by a large majority. If resistance to the Slave Power was the reserved watchword of your first election, the triumphant war cry of your re-election is Death to Slavery.

From the commencement of the titanic American strife the workingmen of Europe felt instinctively that the star-spangled banner carried the destiny of their class. The contest for the territories which opened the dire epopee [the Civil War], was it not to decide whether the virgin soil of immense tracts should be wedded to the labor of the emigrant or prostituted by the tramp of the slave driver?

When an oligarchy of 300,000 slaveholders dared to inscribe, for the first time in the annals of the world, "slavery" on the banner of Armed Revolt, when on the very spots where hardly a century ago the idea of one great Democratic Republic had first sprung up, whence the first Declaration of the Rights of Man [the Declaration of Independence] was issued, and the first impulse given to the European revolution of the eighteenth century [the French Revolution]; when on those very spots counterrevolution, with systematic thoroughness, gloried in rescinding "the ideas entertained at the time of the formation of the old constitution," and maintained slavery to be "a beneficent institution," indeed, the old solution of the great problem of "the relation of capital to labor," and cynically proclaimed property in man "the cornerstone of the new edifice"—then the working classes of Europe understood at once, even before the fanatic partisanship of the upper classes for the Confederate gentry had given its dismal warning, that the slaveholders' rebellion was to sound the tocsin for a general holy crusade of property against labor, and that for the men of labor, with their hopes for the future, even their past conquests were at stake in that tremendous conflict on the other side of the Atlantic. Everywhere they bore therefore patiently the hardships imposed upon them by the cotton crisis, opposed enthusiastically the proslavery intervention of their betters—and, from most parts of Europe, contributed their quota of blood to the good cause.

While the workingmen, the true political powers of the North, allowed slavery to defile their own republic, while before the Negro, mastered and sold without his concurrence, they boasted it the highest prerogative of the white-skinned laborer to sell himself and choose his own master, they were unable to attain the true freedom of labor, or to support their European brethren in their struggle for emancipation; but this barrier to progress has been swept off by the red sea of civil war.

The workingmen of Europe feel sure that, as the American War of Independence initiated a new era of ascendancy for the middle class, so the American Antislavery War will do for the working classes. They consider it an earnest of the epoch to come that it fell to the lot of Abraham Lincoln, the single-minded son of the working class, to lead his country through the matchless struggle for the rescue of an enchained race and the reconstruction of a social world.

Adams to International Workingman's Association, January, 1865.[6]

The Central Council of the International Workingmen's Association presented the letter to the American ambassador Charles Francis Adams, who in turn sent it to the American Secretary of State, William H. Seward. W. R. Cremer, the group's Honorary General Secretary, wrote the ambassador "to ask that you will forward the accompanying address to the President of the United States of America, the sentiments therein expressed being the spontaneously expressed views of the central council, which council but represents the sentiments of the workingmen of Europe."

Lincoln had followed British opinion on the war and on emancipation and understood the importance of worker support for the Union in shaping public. On April 6, 1864, Lincoln had received English abolitionist orator George Thompson at the White House. While there, Thompson told him, "the aristocracy and the money interest were desirous of seeing the Union broken up, but that the great heart of the masses beat in sympathy with the North. They instinctively felt that the cause of liberty was bound up with our success in putting down the Rebellion, and the struggle was being watched with the deepest anxiety."[7] *Adams responded for the President, making clear the abolitionist goal of the Civil War as "the cause of human nature."*

I am directed to inform you that the address of the Central Council of your Association, which was duly transmitted through this Legation to the President of the United States, has been received by him. So far as the sentiments expressed by it are personal, they are accepted by him with a sincere and anxious desire that he may be able to prove himself not unworthy of the confidence which has been recently extended to him by his fellow citizens and by so many of the friends of humanity and progress throughout the world.

The Government of the United States has a clear consciousness that its policy neither is nor could be reactionary, but at the same time it adheres to the course which it adopted at the beginning, of abstaining everywhere from propagandism and unlawful intervention. It strives to do equal and exact justice to all states and to all men and it relies upon the beneficial results of that effort for support at home and for respect and good will throughout the world.

Nations do not exist for themselves alone, but to promote the welfare and happiness of mankind by benevolent intercourse and example. It is in this relation that the United States regard their cause in the present conflict with slavery, maintaining insurgence as the cause of human nature, and they derive new encouragements to persevere from the testimony of the workingmen of Europe that the national attitude is favored with their enlightened approval and earnest sympathies . . . .

Marx to Engels, February 10, 1865.[8]

In a letter to Engels, Marx celebrated the favorable response the International Workingmen's Association received from Lincoln, particularly when compared to that of a bourgeois emancipation society.

The fact that Lincoln answered us so courteously and the "BOURGEOIS EMANCIPATION SOCIETY" so brusquely and purely formally made *The Daily News* so indignant that they did not print the answer to us. However, since they saw, to their dismay, that *The Times* was doing so, they had to publish it *later* in *The Express* . . . . The difference between Lincoln's answer to us and to the bourgeoisie has created such a sensation here that the West End "clubs" are shaking their heads at it. You can understand how gratifying that has been for our people.

LINCOLN ON RECONSTRUCTION

Lincoln, "Second Inaugural Address," March 4, 1865.[9]

While Marx linked the fate of slaves and workers worldwide, Lincoln worked on ways to reconstruct the government, once the Confederacy had surrendered. In the seven hundred words of his poetical and biblical Second Inaugural Address, Lincoln unambiguously deemed slavery the cause of the Civil War. He dubbed that institution the country's original sin and feared that "every drop of blood drawn with the lash shall be paid by another drawn with the sword." He urged the nation to finish the work of slave emancipation, but at the same time, "with malice toward none," he urged a peaceful reconstruction of the southern states.

✳

Fellow-Countrymen: At this second appearing to take the oath of the Presidential office there is less occasion for an extended address than there was at the first.... Now, at the expiration of four years, during which public declarations have been constantly called forth on every point and phase of the great contest which still absorbs the attention and engrosses the energies of the nation, little that is new could be presented. The progress of our arms, upon which all else chiefly depends, is as well known to the public as to myself, and it is, I trust, reasonably satisfactory and encouraging to all....

... [F]our years ago all thoughts were anxiously directed to an impending civil war. All dreaded it, all sought to avert it. While the inaugural address was being delivered from this place, devoted altogether to saving the Union without war, insurgent agents were in the city seeking to destroy it without war—seeking to dissolve the Union and divide effects by negotiation. Both parties deprecated war, but one of them would make war rather than let the nation survive, and the other would accept war rather than let it perish, and the war came.

One-eighth of the whole population were colored slaves, not distributed generally over the Union, but localized in the southern part of it. These slaves constituted a peculiar and powerful interest. All knew that this interest was somehow the cause of the war. To strengthen, perpetuate, and extend this interest was the object for which the insurgents would rend the Union even by war, while the Government claimed no right to do more than to restrict the territorial enlargement of it. Neither party expected for the war the magnitude or the duration which it has already attained. Neither anticipated that the cause of the conflict might cease with or even before the conflict itself should cease. Each looked for an easier triumph, and a result less fundamental and astounding. Both read the same Bible and pray to the same God, and each invokes His aid against the other. It may seem strange that any men should dare to ask a just God's assistance in wringing their bread from the sweat of other men's faces, but let us judge not, that we be not judged [Matt. 7:1]. The prayers of both could not be answered. That of neither has been answered fully. The Almighty has His own purposes. "Woe unto the world because of offenses; for it must needs be that offenses come, but woe to that man by whom the offense cometh [Matt. 18:7]." If we shall suppose that American slavery is one of those offenses which, in the providence of God, must needs come, but which, having continued through His appointed time, He now wills to remove, and that He gives to both North and South this terrible war as the woe due to those by whom the offense came, shall we discern therein any departure from those divine attributes which the believers in a living God always ascribe to Him? Fondly do we hope, fervently do we pray, that this mighty scourge of war may speedily pass away. Yet, if God wills that it continue until all the wealth piled by the bondsman's two hundred and fifty years of unrequited toil shall be sunk, and until every drop of blood drawn with the lash shall be paid by another drawn with the sword, as was said three thousand years ago, so still it must be said "the judgments of the Lord are true and righteous altogether [Ps. 19:9]."

With malice toward none, with charity for all, with firmness in the right as God gives us to see the right, let us strive on to finish the work we are in, to bind up the nation's wounds, to care for him who shall have borne the battle and for his widow and his orphan, to do all which may achieve and cherish a just and lasting peace among ourselves and with all nations.

Lincoln, "Last Public Address," April 11, 1865.[10]

Lincoln wanted to bring the Union back together as soon as possible, on the basis of permanent freedom for all slaves, perhaps allowing "apprenticeships" that would keep former slaves in some kind of unfreedom. Given resistance to national ratification of the Thirteenth Amendment, he was willing to put off discussing, much less insisting upon, suffrage for all freedmen, save perhaps soldiers. In his last public address before his assassination, he commented on Reconstruction in Louisiana and particularly on Salmon P. Chase's desire that "colored loyalists ought to be allowed to participate" in the process—to vote, as he wrote Lincoln the day after he delivered the address.

We meet this evening, not in sorrow, but in gladness of heart. The evacuation of Petersburg and Richmond, and the surrender of the principal insurgent army, give hope of a righteous and speedy peace whose joyous expression can not be restrained.... By these recent successes the re-inauguration of the national authority—reconstruction—which has had a large share of thought from the first, is pressed much more closely upon our attention. It is fraught with great difficulty. Unlike the case of a war between independent nations, there is no authorized organ for us to treat with. No one man has authority to give up the rebellion for any other man. We simply must begin with, and mould from, disorganized and discordant elements. Nor is it a small additional embarrassment that we, the loyal people, differ among ourselves as to the mode, manner, and means of reconstruction....

In ... Dec. 1863 ... , I presented a plan of re-construction ... which, I promised, if adopted by any State, should be acceptable to, and sustained by, the Executive government of the nation. I distinctly stated that this was not the only plan which might possibly be acceptable.... This plan was, in advance, submitted to the then Cabinet, and distinctly approved by every member of it. One of them suggested that I should . . . apply the Emancipation Proclamation to the theretofore excepted parts of Virginia and Louisiana; that I should drop the suggestion about apprenticeship for freed-people . . . ; but even he approved . . . the plan which has since been employed or touched by the action of Louisiana. The new constitution of Louisiana, declaring emancipation for the whole State, practically applies the Proclamation to the part previously excepted. It does not adopt apprenticeship for freed-people . . . . So that, as it applies to Louisiana, every member of the Cabinet fully approved the plan . . . . From about July 1862, I had corresponded with different persons, supposed to be interested, seeking a reconstruction of a State government for Louisiana. When the Message of 1863 . . . reached New-Orleans, Gen. Banks wrote me that he was confident the people, with his military co-operation, would reconstruct, substantially on that plan. I wrote him, and some of them to try it; they tried it, and the result is known. Such only has been my agency in getting up the Louisiana government. As to sustaining it, my promise is out, as before stated . . . .

The . . . constituency . . . on which the new Louisiana government rests, would be more satisfactory to all, if it contained fifty, thirty, or even twenty thousand, instead of only about twelve thousand, as it does. It is also unsatisfactory to some that the elective franchise is not given to the colored man. I would myself prefer that it were now conferred on the very intelligent, and on those who serve our cause as soldiers. Still the question is not whether the Louisiana government, as it stands, is quite all that is desirable. The question is "Will it be wiser to take it as it is, and help to improve it; or to reject, and disperse it?" "Can Louisiana be brought into proper practical relation with the Union sooner by sustaining, or by discarding her new State Government?"

Some twelve thousand voters in the heretofore slave-state of Louisiana have sworn allegiance to the Union . . . , held elections, organized a State government, adopted a free-state constitution, giving the benefit of public schools equally to black and white, and empowering the Legislature to confer the elective franchise upon the colored man. Their Legislature has already voted to ratify the constitutional amendment recently passed by Congress, abolishing slavery throughout the nation. These twelve thousand persons are thus fully committed to the Union, and to perpetual freedom in the state—committed to the very things, and nearly all the things the nation wants—and they ask the nations recognition, and its assistance to make good their committal. Now, if we reject, and spurn them, we do our utmost to disorganize and disperse them. We in effect say to the white men "You are worthless, or worse—we will neither help you, nor be helped by you." To the blacks we say "This cup of liberty which these, your old masters, hold to your lips, we will dash from you, and leave you to the chances of gathering the spilled and scattered contents in some vague and undefined when, where, and how." If this course, discouraging and paralyzing both white and black, has any tendency to bring Louisiana into proper practical relations with the Union, I have, so far, been unable to perceive it. If, on the contrary, we recognize, and sustain the new government of Louisiana the converse . . . is made true. We encourage the hearts, and nerve the arms of the twelve thousand to adhere to their work, and argue for it, and proselyte for it, and fight for it, and feed it, and grow it, and ripen it to a complete success. The colored man too, in seeing all united for him, is inspired with vigilance, and energy, and daring, to the same end. Grant that he desires the elective franchise, will he not attain it sooner by saving the already advanced steps toward it, than by running backward over them? Concede that the new government of Louisiana is only to what it should be as the egg is to the fowl, we shall sooner have the fowl by hatching the egg than by smashing it? Again, if we reject Louisiana, we also reject one vote in favor of the proposed amendment to the national constitution. To meet this proposition, it has been argued that no more than three fourths of those States which have not attempted secession are necessary to validly ratify the amendment. I do not commit myself against this, further than to say that such a ratification would be questionable, and sure to be persistently questioned; while a ratification by three fourths of all the States would be unquestioned and unquestionable . . . .

MARX ON RECONSTRUCTION AND THE AMERICAN PROLETARIAT

Address from the Working Men's International Association to President Johnson, May 1865.[11]

Two or three weeks after Lincoln's assassination, Marx—again writing for the International Workingmen's Association—composed a letter to President Andrew Johnson, lamenting Lincoln's death, the recent sorrow of his avowed enemies, and judging Lincoln as a humble if plodding man who accomplished a great thing while remaining morally upright. He urged Johnson to complete the work of "political reconstruction and social regeneration."

To Andrew Johnson, President of the United States. The demon of the "peculiar institution," for the supremacy of which the South rose in arms, would not allow his worshippers to honourably succumb in the open field. What he had begun in treason, he must needs end in infamy. As Philip II's war for the Inquisition [against the Netherlands] bred a Gerard [assassin of William I of Orange, the Dutch independence leader] thus Jefferson Davis's pro-slavery war a Booth.

It is not our part to call words of sorrow and horror, while the heart of two worlds heaves with emotion. Even the sycophants who, year after year, and day by day, stick to their . . . work of morally assassinating Abraham Lincoln, and the great Republic he headed, stand now aghast at this universal outburst of popular feeling, and rival with each other to strew rhetorical flowers on his open grave. They have now at last found out that he was a man, neither to be browbeaten by adversity, nor intoxicated by success, inflexibly pressing on to his great goal, never compromising it by blind haste, slowly maturing his steps, never retracing them, carried away by no surge of popular favour, disheartened by no slackening of the popular pulse, tempering stern acts by the gleams of a kind heart, illuminating scenes dark with passion by the smile of humour, doing his titanic work as humbly and homely as Heaven-born rulers do little things with the grandiloquence of pomp and state; in one word, one of the rare men who succeed in becoming great, without ceasing to be good. Such, indeed, was the modesty of this great and good man, that the world only discovered him a hero after he had fallen a martyr . . . .

After a tremendous civil war, but which, if we consider its vast dimensions, and its broad scope, and compare it to the Old World's 100 years' wars, and 30 years' wars, and 23 years' wars, can hardly be said to have lasted 90 days. Yours, Sir, has become the task to uproot by the law what has been felled by the sword, to preside over the arduous work of political reconstruction and social regeneration. A profound sense of your great mission will save you from any compromise with stern duties. You will never forget that to initiate the new era of the emancipation of labour, the American people devolved the responsibilities of leadership upon two men of labour—the one Abraham Lincoln, the other Andrew Johnson . . . .

Marx and Engels, however, soon became disillusioned with President Johnson, his resistance to making former slaves into citizens and bringing the southern states back into the Union. In June 1765, Marx wrote Engels that "Johnson's policy likes me not." A month later, Engels agreed, writing Marx that "MR Johnson's policy is less and less to my liking, too. NIGGER [sic] -hatred is coming out more and more violently, and he is relinquishing all his power vis-à-vis the old lords in the South. If this should continue,

all the old secessionist scoundrels will be in Congress in Washington in 6 months time. Without COLOURED SUFFRAGE nothing can be done, and Johnson is leaving it up to the defeated, the ex-slaveowners, to decide on that. It is absurd." Disappointed in the progress of Reconstruction, Marx soon turned attention to the American working class.[12]

Marx, Capital, vol. 1.[13]

In Capital, volume 1, Marx assessed the impact of the Civil War on the American working class, continuing a theme he raised in his letter to President Lincoln. Capitalist corruption, he concluded, had ended opportunities for poor immigrants and increased the immiseration of workers, but had led to a renewed workers' movement, one not possible as long as slavery remained legal.

On the one hand, the enormous and ceaseless stream of men, year after year driven upon America, leaves behind a stationary sediment in the east of the United States, the wave of immigration from Europe throwing men on the labour-market there more rapidly than the wave of emigration westwards can wash them away. On the other hand, the American Civil War brought in its train a colossal national debt, and, with it, pressure of taxes, the rise of the vilest financial aristocracy, the squandering of a huge part of the public land on speculative companies for the exploitation of railways, mines, &c., in brief, the most rapid centralization of capital. The great republic has, therefore, ceased to be the promised land for emigrant labourers. Capitalistic production advances there with giant strides, even though the lowering of wages and the dependence of the wage-worker are yet far from being brought down to the normal European level . . . .

In the United States of North America, every independent movement of the workers was paralysed so long as slavery disfigured a part of the Republic. Labour cannot emancipate itself in the white skin where in the black it is branded. But out of the death of slavery a new life at once arose. The first fruit of the Civil War was the eight hours' agitation, that ran with the seven-leagued boots of the locomotive from the Atlantic to the Pacific, from New England to California. The General Congress of labour at Baltimore (August 16th, 1866) declared: "The first and great necessity of the present, to free the labour of this country from capitalistic slavery, is the passing of a law by which eight hours shall be the normal working day in all States of the American Union. We are resolved to put forth all our strength until this glorious result is attained."

Marx, "Address to the National Labor Union of the United States" May 12, 1869.[14]

In 1869, Marx addressed his "Fellow Workmen" in the United States. He warned them that the ruling class was trying to foment war between Britain and the United States, one that would be detrimental to American workers. After reminding the workers of his address to Lincoln on his reelection, Marx turned to the consequences of the Civil War for working peoples, pointing both to greater poverty and a newly revitalized labor movement.

In a congratulatory address to Mr. Lincoln on his reelection as president, we expressed our conviction that the American Civil War would prove of as great import to the advancement of the working class as the American War of Independence had proved to that of the middle class. And, in point of fact, the victorious termination of the antislavery war has opened a new epoch in the annals of the working class. In the States themselves, an independent working-class movement, looked upon with an evil eye by your old parties and their professional politicians, has since that date sprung into life. To fructify it wants years of peace. To crush it, a war between the United States and England is wanted.

The next palpable effect of the Civil War was, of course, to deteriorate the position of the American workman. In the United States, as in Europe, the monster incubus of a national debt was shifted from hand to hand, to settle down on the shoulders of the working class. The prices of necessaries, says one of your statesmen, have since 1860 risen 78 percent, while the wages of unskilled labor rose 50 percent, those of skilled labor 60 percent only. Pauperism . . . grows now in America faster than population. Moreover, the suffering of the working classes set off as a foil the newfangled luxury of financial aristocrats, shoddy aristocrats, and similar vermin bred by wars. Yet, for all this, the Civil War did compensate by freeing the slave and the consequent moral impetus it gave to your own class movement . . . .

New York Herald *Interview 1871.*[15]

Six years after the Civil War, Marx, in an August 3, 1871, interview with the New York Herald, *compared the fate of slaves and proletarians and listed the revolutionary aims of the first international (communist) organizations. He clearly drew on his research on slavery and his extensive reading about the Civil War and the United States.*

What better is the condition of the man who works for a dollar a day—that is, sells himself for a day at a time for just enough to support life—than that of the Negro slave who is clothed and fed by his master? Capital is, after all, only another form of slavery and the condition of the laborer is the same in either case. Take the arguments used by the former slaveholders in the southern states of America in defense of slavery and you will find them identical with those used by capitalists and monopolists today. "What right have you to compel these Negroes to work for your profit alone when you only give them the bare necessities of life?" The answer is ready—"I bought them . . ."

Correspondent: What are the principal aims of the society in the United States?

Dr. Marx: To emancipate the workingman from the rule of politicians and to combat monopoly in all the many farms it is assuming there, especially that of the public lands. We want no more monstrous land grabs, no more grants to swindling railroad concerns, no more schemes for robbing the people of their birthright for the benefit of a few purse-proud monopolists.

EPILOGUE

Marx and Lincoln after the Defeat of the Paris Commune

HISTORIANS OFTEN INDULGE in counterfactuals, the "what-ifs" of the past. What might have happened if a still-alive Abraham Lincoln and Karl Marx had met in 1871, after Marx suffered through the defeat of the Paris Commune and the victory of the bourgeoisie? Perhaps Marx would have immigrated to New York City, where he could have met Lincoln in a coffeeshop and reminiscence about slavery, the Civil War, and emancipation. Lincoln would have appreciated the support Marx and the Workingmen's International Association had given to him and his policies during the Civil War, along with Marx's understanding of the political constraints that prevented full and quick abolition of slavery. But there their agreement would have ended.

Marx would have told Lincoln that the United States would soon descend to levels common in Europe, with capitalists stealing the hard-earned wages of their workers. Nor would Lincoln's Homestead Act help. The vast quantities of free land, he might remark, would hardly retard such thievery for very long. Lincoln, who championed the Homestead Act, surely would have disagreed—and he would have pointed to the rapid settlement of the plains states, often by poor European immigrants. They would have argued over capital and labor: Lincoln clinging to a vision of the unity of labor and capital, Marx to the inevitable and fierce conflict between them.

Lincoln would remind Marx that as president he had to consider public opinion in the North and the tenacity with which slaveholders and their non-slave-owning supporters clung to slavery. Marx would respond that the Union won the war only when it appeared to treat all workers, white and black, as equal—equal in rights, equal in the exploitation they suffered from slaveholders or capitalists. Lincoln would tell Marx that one could not mandate social equality, and only an easy reconstruction, which would bring back those who had fought for the Confederacy, could protect the human rights of freed slaves. Nor were all workers equal; the condition of the freed people would have improved if most served serve an apprenticeship.

Marx, who understood the necessity of formal equality, shared by white and black workers alike, would surely have lamented the failures of Reconstruction.

Of course, Lincoln had died six years earlier, and Marx never came to the United States. But perhaps we can judge the adequacy of their predictions. Lincoln may have supported ratification of the Fourteenth and Fifteenth Amendments to the Constitution but would not have predicted either the violence of Reconstruction or its repudiation, by the North and South, nearly two decades later. The continuing animosity toward freedmen and women and their descendants, however, would hardly have surprised him. Marx, who lived longer, did accurately predict labor agitation and even the violence that permeated the relations between capitalists and proletarians, rulers and ruled, all over the Western world, including the United States, during the last three decades of the nineteenth century—and deep onto our own century.

Bibliographic Essay

OF WRITING ABOUT the American Civil War and Karl Marx and Abraham Lincoln there is no end. An Atlantic and international perspective stands behind this anthology, one which places ante-bellum and Civil War history in an Atlantic context and thus justifies placing Lincoln and Marx in dialogue. Two articles in the *Journal of the Civil War Era,* David M. Prior, et al., "Teaching the Civil War Era in Global Context: A Discussion," 5 (2015): 97–125, and Douglas R. Egerton, "Rethinking the Atlantic Historiography in a Post-Colonial Era: The Civil War in a Global Perspective," 1 (2011): 75–95, provide introductions. The best full-length study, Don H. Doyle, *The Cause of All Nations: An International History of the American Civil War* (New York: Basic Books, 2015), examines popular and elite opinion about the war in Britain and the Europe.

Very few works connect the Lincoln and Marx. In his *An Unfinished Revolution: Karl Marx and Abraham Lincoln* (London: Verso, 2011), Robin Blackburn, a historian of slavery and abolition, combined Lincoln and Marx documents. His superb introduction links the two analytically and thematically, particularly on issues of labor, slavery, and the Civil War. Perhaps because he deals exclusively with the war years, Blackburn misses Lincoln's vision of the self-made agrarian man, a framework Marx rejects. Several other works connect Lincoln and Marx or deal with Marx and the Civil War. Doyle's *Cause of All Nations* demonstrates that Marx was one of the few European intellectuals who knew from early 1861 that secession and the Civil War concerned slavery. Betsy Erkkila, "Lincoln in International Memory," in Shirley Samuels, ed., *The Cambridge Companion to Abraham Lincoln* (Cambridge: Cambridge University Press, 2012): 155–182, places Marx's writing about Lincoln in a European context. Gerald Runkle analyzed all of Marx and Engels's Civil War writings in "Karl Marx and the American Civil War," *Comparative Studies in Society and History* 6 (January 1964): 117–141, but scholarship over the past half-century has challenged several of his judgments about Marx's accuracy.

Although other works on Lincoln and on Marx at best briefly mention the other, a wealth of material allows students to further explore the topic. The best way to learn more about both is through their writings. Online editions are readily accessible. The Marx-Engels Internet Archive, http://www.marxists.org/archive/marx/, reprints English versions of many of Karl Marx's and Frederick Engels's published works (Engels was Marx's long-time collaborator). The most complete English language edition of their writings, the fifty-volume edition *Karl Marx, Frederick Engels: Collected Works* (London: Lawrence and Wishart and International Publishers, 1975-2004) includes all published works and all of Marx's and Engels's outgoing correspondence. Roy P. Basler edited eight volumes of Lincoln's writings: *Collected Works. The Abraham Lincoln Association, Springfield, Illinois* (New Brunswick, NJ: Rutgers University Press, 1953-1955), online at http://quod.lib.umich.edu/l/lincoln/. (The supplementary volumes, published in 1974 and 1990 are not online.) The Library of Congress has put its vast trove of Lincoln Papers online, http://memory.loc.gov/ammem/alhtml/malhome.html. All outgoing correspondence has been (or will be) transcribed, along with digital images, as will much of the incoming correspondence. The Papers of Abraham Lincoln, http://www.papersofabrahamlincoln.org/, aims at extending the Basler edition.

Printed selections from the works of Marx and Lincoln abound. The most relevant Lincoln collection is *Lincoln on Democracy: His Own Words, with Essays by America's Foremost Civil War Historians*, edited by Mario M. Cuomo and Harold Holzer (New York: Harper Collins, 1990), with chapters on "Lincoln and the American Dream" and "Lincoln and Slavery," both crucial issues in this book. Michael P. Johnson's collection *Abraham Lincoln, Slavery, and the Civil War: Selected Writings and Speeches* (Boston: Bedford-St. Martin's, 2001; 2nd ed. 2011) emphasizes the Civil War and emancipation while including earlier material. Three anthologies cover Marx's writings on the United States and the Civil War: Herbert M. Morais, ed., *The Civil War in the United States: Karl Marx and Frederick Engels* (New York: International Publishers, 1937); Andrew Zimmerman, ed., *The Civil War in the United States: Karl Marx and Frederick Engels* (New York: International Publishers, 2016), a through revision, with different documents than the 1937 edition; Saul Padover, ed., *Karl Marx on America and the Civil War* (New York: McGraw Hill, 1972). Padover's introduction places Marx's writings in the context of his life and theories; Zimmerman's introduction (and texts he selects) places the American Civil War at the center of Marx's thinking about proletarian Revolution.

Those who wish to understand the lives of Marx and of Lincoln have a multitude of biographies from which to choose. For Lincoln, David Herbert Donald's *Lincoln* (New York: Simon & Schuster, 1995), a full biography, stressing the war years, and Orville Vernon Burton, *The Age of Lincoln* (New York: Hill and Wang, 2007), which places Lincoln in broad context and argues that he was a Southerner, provide contrasting readings. David McLellan, *Karl Marx: His Life and Thought* (London: Macmillian, 1973; 4th ed., 2006), examines Marx's vision of the United

States in the context of his politics; economic and political writings; and personal and familial life. Jonathan Sperber, *Karl Marx: A Nineteenth-Century Life* (New York: Liveright, 2013) turns Marx into an Enlightenment figure, influenced by the philosopher Georg Hegel, whose writing and politics harked back to the French Revolution.

Over the past five decades, historians have examined the economic and political contexts in which Marx and Lincoln lived. Debased proletarians, with little more than their labor power to sell, fought capitalists and their political allies all over Britain (where Marx lived in exile starting in 1849) and much of Western Europe. These were the people who Marx attempted to organize and to whom Marx and Frederick Engels aimed their *Communist Manifesto*. The classic examination of the English working class remains Engels, *The Condition of the Working Class in England in 1844*, found at marxists.org. E. P. Thompson's brilliant *The Making of the English Working Class* (New York: Pantheon, 1963), which ends around 1830, serves as a backdrop to Marx and Engels' writings; for the later history of the English working class, see John Foster, *Class Struggle and the Industrial Revolution: Early Industrial Capitalism in Three English Towns* (London: Weidenfeld and Nicolson, 1974), and the sprightly, if contentious, essays by E. J. Hobsbawm in *Labouring Men: Studies in the History of Labour* (New York: Basic Books, 1964).

Both Lincoln and Marx knew that the United States remained an agrarian country, if rent by slavery in the South. Scott Reyonds Nelson, "Who Put Their Capitalism in My Slavery," *Journal of the Civil War Era* 5 (2015): 289–310, examines the fraught historiography of the relationship between slavery and capitalism, central in understanding both Marx and Lincoln. In *Empire of Cotton: A Global History* (New York: Knopf, 2014), Swen Beckert connects the rise of American cotton production, and its dominance in the British textile markets, to slavery, the nearly unlimited number of enslaved workers planters could command. His work provides support for Marx's argument that slave labor sustained British industrial capitalism, but overemphasizes the link between cotton production and economic development, both in Britain and the United States.

Historians have uncovered much evidence that challenges any ideal of social mobility, much less equality, in the countryside. Paul Wallace Gates analyzes US land policy, tenancy, squatting, and conflicts between speculators and settlers in *History of Public Land Law Development. Written for the Public Land Law Review Commission* (Washington, DC: Government. Printing Office, 1968) and *Landlords and Tenants on the Prairie Frontier: Studies in American Land Policy* (Ithaca, NY: Cornell University Press, 1973). The best examination of the northern agricultural economy, Jeremy Atack and Fred Bateman's *To Their Own Soil: Agriculture in the Antebellum North* (Ames: Iowa State University Press, 1987), shows the increasing economic distance between commercial farmers and those struggling for a livelihood. John Mack Faragher's *Sugar Creek: Life on the Illinois Prairie* (New Haven, CT: Yale University Press, 1986) depicts the initial settlement and search for subsistence in a community near Illinois' capital Springfield, while James M. Marshall argues in *Land Fever: Dispossession and the Frontier Myth* (Lexington: University Press of Kentucky, 1986) that as many as a third of all pioneers failed to get land.

Long before 1858, when Lincoln ran for a US Senate seat in Illinois, an urban working class had come to dominate cities such as New York. New York City most resembled Marx's London. The best examination of laboring people in antebellum New York City, Sean Wilentz's *Chants Democratic: New York City and the Rise of the American Working Class, 1788-1850* (New York: Oxford University Press, 1984), emphasizes the debasement of wage labor, the development of a unique system of "metropolitan industrialization," and political conflicts over labor. In an important revisionist study, *Scraping By: Wage Labor, Slavery, and Survival in Early Baltimore* (Baltimore: Johns Hopkins University Press, 2009), Seth Rockman stresses the failure of poor men and women to rise out of poverty and the conflicts between workers and employers there.

Almost no scholarship deals with Marx's views of the United States, and readers seeking a broad understanding of Marx's economic theories and historical arguments run into an impenetrable theoretical works or ideological posturing. The best short introduction is found in John E. Tewes, ed., *The Communist Manifesto by Karl Marx and Frederick Engels with Related Documents* (Boston: Bedford St. Martin's, 1999): 1-53. David Harvey, in *A Companion to Marx's Capital* (London: Verso, 2010), provides clear explanations of volume 1 of *Capital*; readers might pay special attention to chapters 4 and 5 on labor and the working day and chapter 11 on primitive accumulation, those most relevant to understanding Marx's vision of American society. Shlomo Avineri, *The Social and Political Thought of Karl Marx* (Cambridge: Cambridge University Press, 1968) relates Marx's ideas on such issues as the proletariat, alienation, property, and revolution in a comprehensible way. G. A. Cohen, *Karl Marx's Theory of History: A Defence* expanded edition (Princeton, NJ: Princeton University Press, 2000), is more technical, but his chapters on economic structure, productive forces, and base and superstructure explain Marx's key concepts.

Lincoln, as the 1860 Republican candidate, held a particular economic and political ideology, one that privileged the labor of white men and presumed those men could prosper in a free society, one where no one held slaves in bondage. The classic work on the ideology of the early Republican Party is Eric Foner, *Free Soil, Free Labor, Free Men: The Ideology of the Republican Party before the Civil War* (New York: Oxford University Press, 1970).

While Lincoln's economic ideas have received relatively little attention, his views on slavery and emancipation have elicited a large literature. Gabor S. Boritt examines *Lincoln and the Economics of the American Dream* (Urbana: University of Illinois Press, 1978), covering a range of economic issues over his entire adult life. In *Lincoln, Land, and Labor, 1809-60* (Urbana: University of Illinois Press, 1994), Oliver Fraysse analyzes Lincoln's problematic relationship with the land and agrarian life. The most recent, and best, book on Lincoln and slavery is Eric Foner's *The Fiery Trial: Abraham Lincoln and American Slavery* (New York: W. W. Norton, 2010); it makes clear the ambiguities in Lincoln's views and documents the ways they changed from his first exposure to slavery as a youth through the Civil War.

The Civil War, slavery, and emancipation have elicited a sprawling literature. The best one-volume work is still James M. McPherson, *The Battle Cry of Freedom: The Era of the Civil War* (New York: Oxford University Press, 1988); it emphasizes military aspects of the war, but includes chapters dealing with the politics of slavery and with emancipation. McPherson's *Abraham Lincoln and the Second American Revolution* (New York: Oxford University Press, 1990), a sprightly collection of essays, emphasized the radical changes the war brought.

Much like Marx and Lincoln, historians view slavery as the cause of the war and emancipation as its key event. In *The Political Economy of Slavery: Studies in the Economy and Society of the Slave South*, especially chapter 10 (1965; 2nd ed., Middletown, CT: Wesleyan University Press, 1989), Eugene D. Genovese effectively challenged Charles Ramsdel's insistence in "The Natural Limits of Slavery Expansion," *Southwestern Historical Quarterly* 33 (1929): 91-111, that the war was preventable because slavery could not expand beyond its current limits and Charles A. Beard's and Mary R. Beard's argument in *The Rise of American Civilization* (New York: Macmillian, 1927): chapters 17-18, that the Civil War represented a conflict between the agrarian South and an industrial North.

James Oakes's *Freedom National: The Destruction of Slavery in the United States* (New York: W. W. Norton, 2013), examines the political history of emancipation, showing complex maneuvering around emancipation and arguing that both Lincoln and the Republican majority in Congress know that secession and war would inevitably lead to freedom for slaves, as they ran to Union lines. Oakes's *The Scorpion's Sting: Antislavery and the Coming of the Civil War* (New York: W. W. Norton, 2014) places the detailed narrative of *Freedom Nation* in broad temporal and analytical context, showing how only a "cordon of freedom," sustained ultimately by the Thirteenth Amendment—and that neither military emancipation nor the Emancipation Proclamation guaranteed freedom for slaves.

The classic work on the Emancipation Proclamation remains John Hope Franklin, *The Emancipation Proclamation* (Garden City, NY: Doubleday, 1963). Recent work on the making and impact of the Proclamation includes *The Emancipation Proclamation: Three Views* (Baton Rouge: Louisiana State University Press, 2006), with essays about slaves' reaction to the Proclamation (Edna Greene Medford); the legal, political, and military context that surrounded it (Frank J. Williams); and the iconography that enveloped it (Harold Holzer).

In the past several decades, historians have uncovered overwhelming evidence that slaves aided in their own emancipation, by running away, refusing to continue to work, and joining the Union army. A vast literature on slaves and the families and communities they made stands behind these arguments.

The best introductions remain the classic works of Eugene D. Genovese, *Roll, Jordan, Roll: The World the Slaves Made* (New York: Pantheon Books, 1974) and Herbert G. Gutman, *The Black Family in Slavery and Freedom, 1750-1925* (New York: Pantheon Books, 1976).

The most accessible evidence for the impact of war and emancipation on slaves can be found in publications of the Freedmen and Southern Society Project. These include an interpretive history by Ira Berlin et al., *Slaves No More: Three Essays on Emancipation and the Civil War* (Cambridge: Cambridge University Press, 1992) and three document collections, Ira Berlin and Leslie S. Rowland, eds., *Families and Freedom: A Documentary History of African American Kinship in the Civil War Era* (New York: New Press, 1997); Berlin et al. eds., *Free at Last: A Documentary History of Slavery, Freedom, and the Civil War* (New York: New Press, 1992); and Berlin et al., eds., *Freedom's Soldiers: The Black Military Experience in the Civil War* (Cambridge: Cambridge University Press, 1998). Numerous contemporary illustrations of contrabands, black soldiers, and other topics can be found at the American Antiquarian Society's "American Visions of Race, Region, & Reform, in the Press and Letters of Freedmen and Freedmen's Teachers in the Civil War Era," http://www.americanantiquarian.org/Freedmen/.

Notes

Introduction

1. Robin Blackburn, *An Unfinished Revolution: Karl Marx and Abraham Lincoln* (London: Verso, 2011).

2. Jonathan Sperber, *Karl Marx: A Nineteenth-Century Life* (New York: Liveright, 2013): 185-186, 258-259, 273.

3. Eric Foner, *The Fiery Trial: Abraham Lincoln and American Slavery* (New York: W. W. Norton, 2010): 47-51 (Lincoln defending slaveholder); Olivier Fraysse, *Lincoln, Land, and Labor, 1809-1860* (Urbana: University of Illinois Press, 1988): 150-155 (Lincoln and railroads); John E. Tewes, *The Communist Manifesto by Karl Marx and Frederick Engels with Related Documents* (Boston: Bedford St. Martin's, 1999) for Marx's ideas about class conflict.

4. Eric Foner, *Free Soil, Free Labor, Free Men: The Ideology of the Republican Party before the Civil War* (New York: Oxford University Press, 1970).

5. For these ideas, see Abraham Lincoln, "Address before the Wisconsin State Agricultural Society," Milwaukee, September 30, 1859, in Roy P. Basler, ed., *The Collected Works of Abraham Lincoln* (New Brunswick, NJ: Rutgers University Press, 1953-55), 3: 471-482. For the farm ladder, see Gavin Wright, "American Agriculture and the Labor Market: What Happened to Proletarianization?" *Agricultural History* 62 (1988): 182-209.

6. For a summary of these issues, see Allan Kulikoff, *The Agrarian Origins of American Capitalism* (Charlottesville: University Press of Virginia, 1992): chap. 3, esp. 77-95; Fred A. Shannon, "A Post Mortem on the Labor-Safety Valve Theory," *Agricultural History* 19 (1945): 31-37.

7. It is impossible to do more than guess at the number of white abolitionists, but the followers of William Lloyd Garrison provide a clue. There were about 2,500-3,000 subscribers to Garrison's *Liberator*. If half were white, that would suggest some 1,250-1,500 strong white abolitionists. See William E. Cain, ed., *William Lloyd Garrison and the Fight against Slavery: Selections from the Liberator* (Boston: Bedford St. Martin's, 1995): 5.

8. Foner, *Fiery Trial*, 56-59, for Lincoln's bill.

9. Foner, *Fiery Trial*, esp. chap 1.

10. James Oakes, *Freedom National: The Destruction of Slavery in the United States* (New York: W. W. Norton, 2013).

11. Foner, *Fiery Trial*, chap. 4 esp. 69-72, 95-111.

12. Foner, *Fiery Trial*, 8-14, 27-28, and esp. 85.

13. Blackburn, ed., *Unfinished Revolution*, 11.

14. Oakes, *Freedom National*, 49–61, 70–73.

15. Orville Browning, "Senator's Diary Describes Emancipation Evolution," http://housedivided.dickinson.edu/sites/emancipation/2012/11/06/senator-brownings-diary-describes-emancipations-evolution (quote); Oakes, *Freedom National*, chaps. 3–5, gives many examples.

16. Oakes, *Freedom National*, 277–282; Foner, *Fiery Trial*, 224–230; Philip W. Magness and Sebastian N. Page, *Colonization after Emancipation: Lincoln and the Movement for Black Resettlement* (Columbia: University of Missouri Press, 2011), find evidence that Lincoln continued private diplomacy to find a place to resettle slaves for all of 1863.

17. Oakes, *Freedom National*, 176–189, 236–239, 356–359.

18. Ira Berlin et al., *Slaves No More: Three Essays on Emancipation and the Civil War* (Cambridge: Cambridge University Press, 1992); Willie Lee Rose, *Rehearsal for Reconstruction: The Port Royal Experiment* (1964; Athens: University of Georgia Press, 1999).

19. Blackburn, ed., *Unfinished Revolution*, 21–22, 27, 35, 38–39; Gerald Runkle, "Karl Marx and the American Civil War," *Comparative Studies in Society and History* 6 (January 1964): 120, 126, 136–139.

20. The most accessible short collection of *Die Presse* essays is in Blackburn, ed., *Unfinished Revolution*, 151–180.

21. This paragraph and the next two draw on Oakes, *Freedom National*, chaps. 8 and 10, esp. 350–367, 386–390.

22. Berlin et al., *Slaves No More*, chap. 3.

23. Francis Bicknell Carpenter, *Six Months at the White House with Abraham Lincoln: The Story of a Picture* (New York: Hurd and Houghton, 1866): 90.

24. Berlin et al., *Slaves No More*, 202–205; Oakes, *Freedom National*, 419–421.

25. Richard Greenleaf, "British Labor against American Slavery," *Science & Society* 17 (Winter 1953): 42–58.

26. Blackburn, ed., *Unfinished Revolution*, 46–49.

27. Charles Ramsdel, "The Natural Limits of Slavery Expansion," *Southwestern Historical Quarterly* 33 (1929): 91–111; Charles A. Beard and Mary R. Beard, *The Rise of American Civilization* (New York: Macmillan, 1927): chaps. 17–18.

Chapter 1

1. Karl Marx and Frederick Engels, "The Volks-Tribun's Political Economy and Its Attitude towards Young America," *Circular Against Kriege* (1846) in *Karl Marx, Frederick Engels: Collected Works* (London and New York: Lawrence and Wishart and International, 1975–2004): 6: 41–44; Karl Oberman, *Joseph Weydemeyer: Pioneer of American Socialism* (New York: International Publishers, 1947): 31–32.

2. Marx, *Deutsche-Brüsseler-Zeitung*, no. 90, November 11, 1847, *Marx-Engels Works*, 6: 322–23.

3. Engels to Weydemeyer, August 8, 1751, *Marx-Engels Works*, 38: 406; Weydemeyer to Marx and Engels, December 1, 1851, Oberman, *Weydemeyer*, 36.

4. Karl Marx, *The Eighteenth Brumaire of Louis Bonaparte* (1852), trans. Daniel De Leon (Chicago: Charles Kerr, 1913): 21–22.

5. Marx to Joseph Weydemeyer in New York. London, March 5, 1852, *Marx-Engels Works*, 39: 58.

6. Marx, *Value, Price and Profit*: chap XII. *General Relation of Profits, Wages, and Prices* (1865), https://www.marxists.org/archive/marx/works/1865/value-price-profit/ch03.htm, in English.

7. Lincoln, "Address before the Wisconsin State Agricultural Society," Milwaukee, September 30, 1859, Basler, ed., *Collected Works*, 3: 471–482.

8. "Speech on the Admission of Kansas, Under the Lecompton Constitution, Delivered in the Senate of the United States, March 4, 1858," *Selections from the Letters and Speeches of the Hon. James H. Hammond of South Carolina* (New York: John F. Trow and Com, 1866): 301–322, quotes on 318–320.

9. Oberman, *Weydemeyer*, 95 (first quote); Cincinnati German Workmen to Abraham Lincoln, February 1861, American Memory, d0759100.rft (second quote).

10. Lincoln, "Speech to Germans at Cincinnati, Ohio," February 12, 1861, *Cincinnati Daily and Commercial Gazette* February 13, 1861, Basler, ed., *Collected Works*, 4: 201–203.

11. Lincoln, "1863 Annual Message to Congress," December 8, 1863, Basler, ed., *Collected Works*, 7: 46–47.

12. "A Criticism of American Affairs," *Die Presse*, August 4, 1862, *Marx-Engels Works*, 19: 226.

13. Marx, *Theories of Surplus Value*, chap. 12, https://www.marxists.org/archive/marx/works/1863/theories-surplus-value/ch12.htm.

14. Marx to Engels, November 26, 1869, *Marx-Engels Works*, 43: 383; "The International—Dr. Marx and the *New York Herald* Correspondent in Consultation," *New York Herald*, August 3, 1871.

Chapter 2

1. Lincoln to Mary Speed, September 27, 1841, Basler, ed., *Collected Works*, 1: 260.

2. Lincoln to Joshua F. Speed, August 24, 1855, Basler, ed., *Collected Works*, 2: 320–323.

3. Marx to Pavel Vasilyevich Annenkov, December 28, 1846, *Marx-Engels Works*, 38: 101–102.

4. Karl Marx and Frederick Engels, *Neue Rheinische Zeitung Revue*, May–October 1850, https://www.marxists.org/archive/marx/works/1850/11/01.htm; Oberman, *Weydemeyer*, 50–51.

5. Marx to Engels, June 14, 1853, *Marx-Engels Works*, 39: 345–346.

6. Map: http://www.loc.gov/item/2003627003; Susan Schulten, "The Cartography of Slavery and the Authority of Statistics," *Civil War History*, 56 (2010): 5–32, esp. 16–17 (quote on 16), provides context.

7. Lincoln, "1854 Speech at Peoria," Basler, ed., *Collected Works*, 2: 250–275.

8. Lincoln, "A House Divided," Springfield, Illinois June 16, 1858, Basler, ed., *Collected Works*, 2: 461–462.

9. Marx to Engels, January 11, 1860, *Marx-Engels Works*, 41: 4–5.

10. Karl Marx, "The North American Civil War," *Die Presse*, no. 293, October 25, 1861, *Marx-Engels Works*, 19: 39–40.

11. Karl Marx, *Capital: A Critical Analysis of Capitalist Production*, Samuel Moore and Edward Aveling, trans. (Chicago: Chares Kerr, 1909): 260.

12. Marx, *Capital*, 219, 484–485, 833.

13. Marx, *Capital*, 292, 655.

14. Marx, *Capital*, 593.

Chapter 3

1. Lincoln to Lyman Trumbull, December 10, 1860; Lincoln to William Kellogg, December 11, 1860; Lincoln to Thurlow Weed, December 17, 1760, Basler, ed., *Collected Works*, 4: 149–150, 154.

2. David E. Woodard, "Abraham Lincoln, Duff Green, and the Mysterious Trumbull Letter," *Civil War History* 42 (1996): 211–219, alerted me to these issues. For the letter, see Duff Green to James Buchanan, December 28, 1860, in George T. Curtis, *The Life of James Buchanan* (New York: Harper and Brothers, 1883), 2: 426; the *New York Herald* interview is reprinted in Green, *Acts and Suggestions, Biographical, Historical Financial and Political, Addressed to the People of the United States*. (New York: Richardson, 1866): 226–231.

3. Lincoln to Duff Green, December 28, 1860, Basler, ed., *Collected Works*, 4: 162–163; Woodard, "Lincoln, Green, and the Mysterious Trumbull Letter," 211–219.

4. Woodard, "Lincoln, Green, and the Mysterious Trumbull Letter," 217.

5. Lincoln, "First Inaugural Address—March 4, 1861," Basler, ed., *Collected Works*, 4: 262–271.

6. Marx to Engels, July 5, 1861, *Marx-Engels Works*, 41: 305–307.

7. Karl Marx, "The American Question in England," *New-York Daily Tribune*, October 11, 1861.

8. *Independent*, June 13, 1861, and *Standard*, June 22, 1861. Reprinted in *The War in America: Its Origin and Object. By the Rev. G. H. Shanks. Together with A Letter, addressed to Lord Shaftesbury, by Mrs. Harriet Beecher Stowe*, https://www.harrietbeecherstowecenter.org/worxcms_published/home_page690.shtml.

9. Marx, "The North American Civil War," *Die Presse*, no. 293, October 25, 1861, *Marx-Engels Works*, 19: 32–42.

10. Henry Cleveland, *Alexander H. Stephens, in Public and Private: With Letters and Speeches, Before, During, and Since the War* (Philadelphia: National Publishing, 1886): 717–729, quotes on 721.

11. Marx, "The Civil War in the United States," *Die Presse*, November 7, 1861, *Marx-Engels Works*, 19: 43–44, 49–52.

Chapter 4

1. "The Stampede from Hampton," *Harper's Weekly*, August 17, 1861, 527; illustration on 524.

2. Marx, "The Crisis Over the Slavery Issue," *Die Presse*, no. 343, December 14, 1861, *Marx-Engels Works*, 19: 115–116.

3. Lincoln, "Message to Congress, March 6, 1862," Basler, ed., *Collected Works*, 5: 145.

4. Marx, "A Treaty Against the Slave Trade," *Die Presse*, May 22, 1862, *Marx-Engels Works*, 19: 202–203.

5. Lincoln, "Emancipation Proclamation—First Draft, July 22, 1862," Basler, ed., *Collected Works*, 5: 336–337.

6. Schulten, "The Cartography of Slavery," 6–8, 19–28; Edwin Hergesheimer, composer and Thomas Leonhardt, engraver, "Map Showing the Distribution of the Slave Population of the Southern States of the United States Compiled from the Census of 1860" (Washington: Henry S. Graham, 1861), https://www.loc.gov/item/ody0314/.

7. Marx, "A Criticism of American Affairs," *Die Presse*, August 9, 1862, *Marx-Engels Works*, 19: 226–229.

8. Marx to Engels, August 7, 1862, *Marx-Engels Works*, 41: 400.

9. Lincoln, "Address on Colonization to a Deputation of Negroes," August 14, 1862, *New York Daily Tribune*, August 15, 1862.

10. [Frederick Douglass], "The President and His Speeches," *Douglass' Monthly*, September 1862, 707–708.

11. Lincoln to Horace Greeley, August 22, 1862, Basler, ed., *Collected Works*, 5: 388–389.

12. "Reply to Emancipation Memorial Presented by Chicago Christians of All Denominations," September 13, 1862, Basler, ed., *Collected Works*, 5: 419–424; Foner, *Fiery Trial*, 227–228 (Phillips quote).

Chapter 5

1. Carpenter, *Six Months at the White House*, 20–23, 90, 204–205.
2. Lincoln, "Preliminary Emancipation Proclamation," September 22, 1862, Basler, ed., *Collected Works*, 5: 433–436.
3. Carpenter, *Six Months at the White House*, 90.
4. Marx, "Comments on North American Events," *Die Presse*, October 12, 1862, *Marx-Engels Works*, 19: 248–251.
5. Ephraim Douglass Adams, *Great Britain and the American Civil War* (New York: Longmans, Green, 1925), 2: chap. 12, quote on 102–103.
6. Marx to Engels, October 29, 1862, *Marx-Engels Works*, 41: 420–421.
7. [The Election Results in the Northern States], *Die Presse*, November 23, 1862, *Marx-Engels Works*, 19: 263–264.
8. Marx to Lion Philips, November 29, 1864, *Marx-Engels Works*, 42: 46.
9. John Tenniel, "Abe Lincoln's Last Card; Or, Rouge-et-Noir (Red and Black)," *Punch*, October 18, 1862, 161, http://americanhistory.si.edu/changing-america-emancipation-proclamation-1863-and-march-washington-1963/1863/lincoln-and; *London Times*, October 6, 1862.
10. "Miscegenation Ball," http://loc.gov/pictures/resource/cph.3a17085/; for the two prints mentioned, with their texts, see Ta-Neshisi Coates, "The Miscegenation Ball," *The Atlantic*, June 14, 2010, http://www.theatlantic.com/national/archive/2010/06/the-miscegenation-ball/58149/.
11. Lincoln, "The Emancipation Proclamation," January 1, 1863, Baser, *Collected Works*, 6: 28–31.
12. Lincoln to Major General John A. McClelland, January 8, 1863, Basler, ed., *Collected Works*, 6: 48–49.
13. Thomas Nast, "Emancipation," *Harper's Weekly*, January 24, 1863, http://files.umwblogs.org/blogs.dir/2117/files/2009/04/emancipation100.jpg; 1865 version: http://housedivided.dickinson.edu/sites/emancipation/2011/07/08/thomas-nasts-emancipation-1865/; Barry Schwartz, *Abraham Lincoln and the Forge of National Memory* (Chicago: University of Chicago Press, 2000): 84–85.
14. Lincoln to Nathaniel P. Banks, November 5, 1863, Basler, ed., *Collected Works*, 7: 1–2.
15. Lincoln, "Annual Message to Congress," December 8, 1863, Basler, ed., *Collected Works*, 7: 49–51.
16. Lincoln to Henry C. Wright, December 20, 1863, Basler, ed., *Collected Works*, 7: 81.
17. Lincoln to Mary Tyler Peabody Mann, April 5, 1864, and Mann's response, Basler, ed., *Collected Works*, 7: 287.
18. Lincoln, "Address at Sanitary Fair," Baltimore, Maryland," Basler, ed., *Collected Works*, 7: 301–302, April 18, 1864.
19. "Response to a Serenade," February 1, 1865, *New-York Tribune*, Basler, ed., *Collected Works*, 8: 254–255.

Chapter 6

1. Marx, "A London Workers' Meeting," *Die Presse*, February 2, 1862, *Marx-Engels Works*, 19: 153–156.

2. *New-York Daily Tribune*, February 1, 1862; Adams, *Great Britain and the Civil War*, 2: 107–112.

3. Charles Francis Adams to William H. Seward, October 3, 1862, *Foreign Relations of the United States*, 1862: 205.

4. Karl Marx, "Inaugural Address of the International Working Men's Association," The First International, October 21-27, 1864, in *Inaugural Address and Provisional Rules of the International Working Men's Association*, http://www.marxists.org/archive/marx/works/1864/10/27.htm.

5. *The Bee-Hive Newspaper*, no. 169, November 7, 1865, https://www.marxists.org/archive/marx/iwma/documents/1864/lincoln-letter.htm.

6. Ambassador Adams Replies, Legation of the United States, London, January 28, 1865, *United States Congressional Serial Set*, 1244: 63–64.

7. Carpenter, *Six Months at the White House*, 85–86.

8. Marx to Engels, February 10, 1865, *Marx-Engels Works*, 42: 86.

9. Lincoln, "Second Inaugural Address," March 4, 1865, Basler, ed., *Collected Works*, 8: 332–333.

10. Lincoln, "Last Public Address," April 11, 1865, Basler, ed., *Collected Works*, 8: 399–405.

11. "Address from the Working Men's International Association to President Johnson," written May 2-9, 1865, *The Bee-Hive Newspaper*, May 20, 1865, http://www.marxists.org/archive/marx/iwma/documents/1865/johnson-letter.htm.

12. Marx to Engels, June 24, 1865 and Engels to Marx, July 15, 1865, *Marx-Engels Works*, 42: 163, 167; Andrew Zimmerman, ed. *The Civil War in the United States: Karl Marx and Friedrich Engels* (New York: International Publishers, 2016): xxiv-xxvi, 167-175.

13. Marx, *Capital*, 1: 847 (first selection), 329 (second selection).

14. Marx for the The International Workingmen's Association, "Address to the National Labor Union of the United States" May 12, 1869, https://www.marxists.org/history/international/iwma/documents/1869/us-labor.htm.

15. "The International—Dr. Marx and the *New York Herald* Correspondent in Consultation," *New York Herald*, August 3, 1871. Marx repudiated the interview, but the sentiments on the U.S. therein comport fully with his opinions. See *Marx-Engels Works*, 22: 395.

Illustration Credits

IMAGES

Introduction

Image 1: Bidarchiv pressischer Kulturbesitz, Berlin/ Beard/ Art Resource, NY
Image 2: Chicago Historical Society, ICHi-52428

Chapter 2

Image 1: Library of Congress Prints and Photographs Division, Washington, DC, http://hdl.loc.gov/loc.gmd/g3701e.ct000604

Chapter 4

Image 1: Library of Congress Prints and Photographs Division, Washington, DC, LC-DIG-ppmsca-35556
Image 2: Library of Congress Prints and Photographs Division, Washington, DC, http://hdl.loc.gov/loc.gmd/g3861e.cw0013200

Chapter 5

Image 1: *Punch*, October 18, 1862
Image 2: Library of Congress Prints and Photographs Division, Washington, DC, LC-DIG-ds-06469
Image 3: *Harper's Weekly*, January 24, 1863
Image 4: Library of Congress Prints and Photographs Division, Washington, DC, LC-DIG-pga-03898

Index

Note: Page numbers with documents and illustrations are italicized.

Abe Lincoln's Last Card (John Tenniel), *89–90*
abolitionism: and Civil War, 11, 49, 54, 58, 62, 70, *72–73, 78–79*, 88, 92, 93; gradual abolition, 6, 9–13, 67–68, 82; Lincoln, 9, 13, 32, *94–97*, 106; Marx, 11, 15, *55–57*, 88; militant abolitionism, 8, 15; Republican Party, 7, 9, 15, 87, 88
abolitionists, 1, 6, 9, 12–13, 15, 30, 32, 38, 54, *78–79*, 88, 98, 106, 125n7
Adams, Charles Francis, 1, 13, 14, 55, 102, 104, *104–7*
Adams, John, 55
African slave trade, 11, *38–40*, 60, 68
agricultural productivity, 22
agriculture, in the United States, works on, 121
Alabama, 91
Alexander, Tsar, 42
American cities, works on, 122
American Party. *See* Know-Nothings
American Revolution, *123*
Antietam (Maryland), battle of, 12, 81, 82, *85–87*
anti-slavery sentiments, 31, 36, 88
apprenticeship. *See* emancipation
Arkansas, 61, 91, 96
Atlantic slave trade. *See* African slave trade
Atlantic world, ix, 1, 8, 119

Banks, Nathaniel P., *94*
Beard, Charles, 15
Beard, Mary, 15
Booth, John Wilkes, *112*
Border States, 9–12, 32, 38, 44, 46, 49, 53, 61–62, 67–69, 71–72, 77, 79, 82, 86–87, 92–93, 96
Brazil, 8, 68
Brown, John, 42
Browning, Orville, 9
Brownson, Orestes, 63
Buchanan, James, *59–60*

Bull Run, battle of, 79
Butler, Benjamin F., 79

Cairnes, John Elliot, 104
capitalism: and agriculture, 5, 23–24, 28–29, 36, 42; and industrial revolution, 4, 18, *19*, 33–34, 44; and labor systems, ix, 4–6, 8–11, 13–14, 17, 18, 22, 33, 43–44, *102–4*, 113–15; works on, 121–22
Carey, Henry, 29, 35
Carpenter, Francis Bicknell, 70, 81, *84*
Catholics, 31, 32
Central America, 6, *75*
Chase, Salmon P., 109
child labor, *44*
Cincinnati Daily Commercial, 26
Civil War: black soldiers in, *96*, 96, Union blockade, 13, *100–1*, 102; economic consequences, 113–14; global significance, ix, 1, 4; military necessity emancipation, 92; recruitment, 72; slavery as cause, 8, 11, 15, 54, 73, 80, *107*; slavery during war, 9–10, 92; works on, 122–23
class conflict, 4–5, 14, *102*, 113–15
Cochrane, John, 66
colonization (of freed slaves), 6, 9–10, 16, 39, *74–80*, 82, 126n16
Communist Manifesto, 4
compromise of 1820. *See* Missouri Compromise
compromise of 1850, 38, *38–39*
Confederacy, 10–13, 14–15, 49, 59, 61–62, 70, 86–87, 92, 97, 116
Confiscation Acts, 10–11
contrabands, 9–11, 13, *64–66*, *77–78*
cornerstone speech (Alexander Stephens), *58–59, 104–5*
cotton, 8, 15, 35, 42–43, 70, 100, *103*, *105*
Cremer, W. R., 106

133

Crittenden resolutions (pro-slavery constitutional amendments), *47–48*
crop yields, *22*
Cuba, 68
Curtis, Samuel, *57*

Davis, Jefferson, *112*
Declaration of Independence, *7, 31, 39, 105*
Delaware, *39, 61, 88*
Democratic Party, 5, 17, *53–54, 56,* 59, 62–63, 88–89
Die Presse, 11, 28, *42–43, 58–63,* 64, *66–68, 70–72, 85–87, 100–1*
diplomacy:1862 Atlantic slave trade treaty, 11, 68; British conservatives and Confederacy, 49, *54–59, 89–90, 100*; British workers and the Union, *100–4*; US and Great Britain, *53, 101–2, 106–7*
Distribution of Slave Population (map), *71*
District of Columbia, 11, *39, 84*
Dix, John Adams, 66
Douglas, Stephen, 1, *46–47*
Douglass, Frederick, *76–77*
Dred Scott decision, *41, 56,* 59

economist, *35, 55–58*
elections: 1856, 7, 36, 56; 1858, 7, 15, *41–42*; 1860, 1–2, 3, 6, 15, *42,* 88; 1862, 16, *81, 87*; 1864, 89, *104–6*
emancipation: apprenticeship after emancipation, 6, *92, 94, 110, 116–17*; attacks on, *89–93*; in the British West Indies, *63*; Emancipation Proclamation, *69–70, 81–85, 90–97*; gradual emancipation, *66–68, 92, 94, 110*; military emancipation, 9–11, *66, 70, 92*; self-emancipation, ix, 10–13, *94*; works on, *122–24*
Emancipation, 1863 and 1865, (Thomas Nast print), *93, 95*
Emancipation Proclamation, ix, 1, 4, 9–16, *69–70, 77–78, 81–99, 110*
Engels, Frederick, 2, 4, 13, 15, *18–20, 29, 33, 34–35, 42, 53–54, 73, 87, 107, 112*
Evans, George, 17

family farms, *21–24*
farm ladder, 5, 17, *23–24*
farmers in the United States, 17
filibustering (pro-slavery southerners invasions of Central America), *47*
First Communist International, 29
First Reading of the Emancipation Proclamation (Carpenter), 70, 81
Florida, *91*
Fort Sumter, 56, 59
Fortress Monroe, *64–65*

free blacks, 12
free labor ideology, *23–26*
free soil ideology, *122*
freedom national, *7, 123*
Fremont, John C., 9, 36, 66
French Revolution, 105
Fugitive Slave Act, 9–10, 38, 46, *47, 49,* 52, 59, 72, *83–84*

Garrison, William Lloyd, 9, 125n7
General Congress of labor, *113–14*
Georgia, 70, *91*
German immigrants, *7, 25–26, 70, 77*
Greeley, Horace, 12, *77–78*
Green, Duff, 15, *47–49*

Haiti, 6
Haley's Comet, Papal Bull against, *78*
Halleck, Henry, 66
Hammond, James Henry, 5, 23
Hampton, Virginia, 64, *65–66*
Harper's Ferry, Virginia, 42
Harper's Weekly, 64, *65–66, 93, 95*
Hergesheimer, Edwin, *70, 71*
Homestead Act of 1862, 4–6, 17, *26–27,* 28, 116

Illinois, 9, 22, 60, 88
immigration, *7, 25–26, 77*
Industrial Revolution. *See* capitalism
internal slave trade, 6, *30–33*
International Workingmen's Association, 13, *102–4, 111–13,* 116
Iowa, *57, 60, 88*

Jackson, Andrew, 5
Jay, John, 36
Jefferson, Thomas, *5, 55*
Johnson, Andrew, 14, *111–13*

Kansas, 32, 38, *56, 60*
Kansas-Nebraska Act, 31, 32, 36, *38–39, 56, 59*
Kellogg, William, *46–47*
Kentucky, 9, *30–31, 39, 61, 66, 86–87*
Know-Nothings, 31, 32
Kreige, Hermann, 17, *18–19*

labor power, *4–5*
labor systems: free labor, 4, 14, 17, *23–26*; slavery, ix, *7–8,* 12, 14, *73, 102–4*; under capitalism, 1, *4–5,* 8–11, *13–14,* 17, 22, 33, *43–44, 100–4, 113–15*
land policies, United States, 18, *18–20, 25–27*
land prices, 5
land systems, 5–6, 17, *18–20, 25–27*
Liberia, 6, *38, 73*
Lieber, Francis, 12

Lincoln, Abraham: Address at Sanitary Fair, 98; Address on Colonization, 73–79; agricultural improvement, 21–22; and slavery, 6–7, 9, 30–33, 36–41, 73; Annual Messages, 1862–1863, 12, 27, 94–97; anti-slavery and abolitionist sentiments, 31, 32, 80, 105, 108–9; assassination of, 14; book farming and education, 24; Civil War and slavery, 8–11, 12–15, 53, 56, 80, 83–84, 108–9; Civil War military strategy, 70, 70–72, 78–80, 92–93, 94–97; class origins, 14; colonization, 10, 73–79, 126n16; Crittenden pro-slavery constitutional amendments, 47–48; Declaration of Independence, 31, 39; Emancipation Memorial by Chicago clergy, 78–79; Emancipation Proclamation, 69–70, 81–99, 110; family farms, 24; First Inaugural Address, 15, 49–53; Germans and, 25–26; gradual emancipation, 66–68, 82, 92–93; Homestead Act, 4–6, 27–28; House Divided speech, 8, 15, 41; and Karl Marx, x, 1–4, 116–17; labor and capital, 4–5, 23–24; land and agriculture, 17; liberty, 98; machines in agriculture, 21–22, maps used for military strategy, 70; Peoria speech, 15, 36–37, 36–38; perpetual union, 50–51; property and capital, 14; racial attitudes, 8, 30–31, 39, 73–79, 92–93; the rail splitter, 2–3; Reconstruction, 107–11; Response to a Serenade, 98–99, Second Inaugural Address, 107–9; self-government, 40, 53; slavery expansion, 8, 32, 36–41, 46–50; succession, 50–53, Thirteenth Amendment, 84, 97, 98, 109; US Senate nomination, 7; voting for blacks, 110–11; Wisconsin Agricultural Society Address, 15, 17, 21–24; works by and about, 119–24
Lincoln-Douglas debates, 7
London Times, 85–86, 89, 102
London Trades Council, 13
Louisiana, 16, *91*, 94
Louisville, 32

Mann, Horace, 97
Mann, Mary Peabody, *97–98*
maps, census and Civil War, ix–x, 36, 37, 70, 71
maps of slavery and US censuses, 36, 37, 70, 71
Marx, Karl: 1862 election, 87–88; 1864 Address to International Workingmen's Association, 102–3; and Abraham Lincoln, x, 1–4, 13–14, 70, 86–87, 104–7, 112, 116–17; Address to National Labor Union (US), 114; agricultural commodities, 42; American opportunity, 28, 113–14; Andrew Johnson, *111–13*; on British workers' support for Union, 100–2, 106; capitalism, 14, 33–34, 43–44, 113–14; *Capital*, 8, 15, 33, 43–44, 113–14; Civil War and slavery, 9, 15, 53, *53–63*, 66, 70–72, 86–87, 105; class relations, 17, 20–21, 23, 33, 60, 100–2, 106; *Communist Manifesto*, 4; cotton and slavery, 33–34, 43, 44; *Eighteenth-Brumaire*, 20–21; on Emancipation Proclamation, 85–89; exploitation, 23; and Frederick Engels, 2, 29, 42, 53–54, 87, 107; Henry Carey, 29; Hermann Kriege, *18*; Homestead Act, 26; Letter on Lincoln's reelection, *104–7*; in London, 2, journalism, 13, 15, 28, 42–43, 53–62, 66–68, 70–72, 85–89, 100–2; London Workers' meeting, 1862, 100–2; *New York Herald* interview, 130n15; opportunity in the United States, 20; pauperism in the United States, 19; plantation system, 28; pro-Confederate British press, 54–56, 86, 102; proletarian revolution, 29; proletarians in Britain and Europe, 14, 15–16, 102; proletarians and slavery, 14, 100–2, 104; racial attitudes, 8, 70, 74, 87–88, 113; secession, 53–54; and slavery, 6–8, 12, 16, 32, 33–34, 43, 104; slavery in the territories, 56, slaves as commodities, 45, slave power, 56, slaveholders' revolution, 10–11, 13, 28, 55–62, 87, 101, 105; slaves and proletarians, *114–15;* surplus value, 23; US labor relations post-Civil War, *113–15*, wage slavery, 4, 14, 23, *113–15*; US land system, 5–6; works by and about, 119–22
Maryland, 9, 39, 61, 99
Massachusetts, 88
McClelland, George B., 64, 92
Mexican-American War, 36, 38
Michigan, 60, 88
Miscegenation Ball, 89, 91
Mississippi, 57, 91, 96
Mississippi River, 60, 70
Missouri, 9, 11, 39, 61, 66, 96
Missouri Compromise (1820), 32, 36, 38–39
Morrill, Justin Smith. *See* Morrill Land Grant Act
Morrill Land Grant Act (1862), 4
"mud-sill" theory, 5, 23–24

Nashville Convention, 46
Nast, Thomas, 93, 95
National Reform Association, 17
natural rights, 7
Nebraska, *38–40*
New England, 72
New Orleans, 79
New York City, 87, 116
New York (state), 88
New York Herald, 48, 49, 64–66, 114–15, 130n15
New-York Tribune, 3, 11, 15, 54–58, 78, 98, *100*

North Carolina, 61, 91
Northwest (US region), 61, 72, 88–89
Northwest Ordinance, 38

Ohio, 88
Ohio River, 32

parable of the horse thief (Frederick Douglass), 76–77
parable of the sheep and wolf (Lincoln), 98
Pennsylvania, 88
Philips, Lion, 88–89
Phillips, Wendell, 78
political equality, 25
Pope Callixtus III, 78
Popular Sovereignty, 46
population. *See* slave demography
population growth, 18, 61
Prayer of the Twenty Millions, 77
proletarian revolution, 5
proletariat, 2, 5–6, 14, 18, 21, 33, 102–3, 122
Proudhon, Pierre-Joseph, 33, *33–34*
public lands, United States, 24–26
Punch, 89, 90

race. *See* Lincoln, Abraham; Marx, Karl; Racism
Racism, 73–79, 84, 87–90, 113
Radical Republicans, 13, 14
Ramsdell, Charles, 15
reconstruction (of rebellious states), 16, 116–17
Republican Party, 6–7, 11, 40–41, 46, 88–90
revolutions of 1848, ix, 70
Reynolds's Political Map of the United States, 36, *37*
Roberts, Joseph Jenkins, 75–76

"safety valve" (for waged workers), 5
Saturday Review (London), 55, 86
secession, 9, 10–11, 13, 15, 43, 46–53, 57–59, 61–63, 70, 83
"self-made man," 14
Senate. *See* United States Senate
Seward, William, 15, 82, 102, *106*
Shaftesbury, Lord (Anthony Ashley-Cooper), 54
Shepley, George Foster, 94
Sherman, William Tecumseh, 66
Singleton, Otho R., 57
slave breeding, 43–44
slave catchers, 9
slave demography, 8, 36, *37*, 70, *71*
slave power, 36
slave refugees, 10, 13, 64–66, 78
slaveholders, 7–11, 36
slavery: and capitalism, 8, 43–44, 104–5; in the Civil War, 9, 15, 53, 54–62, 73–74, 78–79, 122–23; and Constitution, 9–10; contrabands, 9–10, 13; emancipation of slaves, 66–68, *70*; ideology of, 6–7, *104–5*; irrepressible conflict thesis, 15; natural limits thesis, 15, *123*; origins of, *39*; politics of, 6–7, 9–10, 14–15, 36–41, 51–63, 73–79, 122–23; slave community and culture, 6–8, 12, *30–31*, 65–66, 93, 94; in the US territories, 8, 10–11, 36, *36–41*, 46–47, 56, *57*, 59–61; and wage labor, 14
South Carolina, 53, 66, 70, 91
Speed, Joshua, *30–33*
Speed, Mary, *30–32*
St. Louis, *30–32*
Stampede of Slaves from Hampton to Fortress Monroe, 64–66
staple agriculture, 42
Stephens, Alexander, 58–59
Stowe, Harriet Beecher, 54
sugar, 8, 42
Sumner, Charles, 68

Tennessee, 54, 61, 96
Tenniel, John, 89
Thayer, Eli, 47
Thirteenth Amendment, US Constitution, 4, 9, 13, 84, 98, 109
Thompson, George, 106
Times on London, 85–86, 89, *102*
Tobacco, 42
Trumbull, Lyman, 46, 48
Tsar Alexander, 42

Union army: Act to Suppress Rebellion, 83–84; Articles of War, 83; military emancipation, 9–11, 67, 70, 72, 92; slave and free black enlistment in, 12–13, 93–97
United States Census, 36, *37*, 70, *71*
United States Constitution, 4, 9–10, 49–52, 55
United States Senate, 7, 60–61

Virginia, *39*, 54, 61, 91
Voting, blacks, 110–11

wage slavery, 4–5, 14, 23
Walker, LeRoy Pope, 59
Washington, George, 55
West Indies, 8, 63
West Virginia, 72
Weydemeyer, Joseph, 20, 33–34
Whig Party, 5, 7, 31, 32
William I of Orange, *112*
Wilmot, David, 7, 31
Wilmot Proviso, 7, 32, 38
Wisconsin State Agricultural Society, 15, 17, 21–24
working class. *See* proletariat

www.ingramcontent.com/pod-product-compliance
Ingram Content Group UK Ltd.
Pitfield, Milton Keynes, MK11 3LW, UK
UKHW021135240326
469240UK00020B/143